WITHDRAWN

Becoming Melungeon

Becoming Melungeon

Making an Ethnic Identity
in the Appalachian South

MELISSA SCHRIFT

University of Nebraska Press • Lincoln & London

Library of Congress Cataloging-in-Publication Data
Schrift, Melissa, 1968–
Becoming Melungeon : making an ethnic identity in
the Appalachian South / Melissa Schrift.
p. cm.
Includes bibliographical references and index.
ISBN 978-0-8032-7154-8 (cloth : alk. paper)
1. Melungeons—Appalachian Mountains,
Southern—Ethnic identity. 2. Melungeons—
Appalachian Mountains, Southern—History.
3. Melungeons—Appalachian Mountains,
Southern—Social conditions. I. Title.
E184.M44S37 2013
305.8'05074—dc23   2012038654

Set in Iowan by Laura Wellington.

In memory of mentor and friend, Nina Etkin

CONTENTS

ACKNOWLEDGMENTS

I have benefitted from a wide and varied amount of support in writing this book. First and foremost I would like to thank my colleagues and students at East Tennessee State University (ETSU), with particular appreciation for the intellectual volley with colleagues Tony Cavender, Lindsey King, Bill Duncan, Joseph Baker, and Amber Kinser. I also appreciate the efforts of chairs, Martha Copp and Leslie McCallister, and Dean Gordon Anderson. This project has greatly benefitted from generous internal research support from ETSU. The character of the university and the cultural richness and beauty of Appalachia remind me daily that my choice to return to the region was the correct one.

I also greatly appreciate the research support from Marquette University, my prior stomping grounds. During my time at Marquette I was active in a small writing group whose members deserve a long overdue thank you: Molly Doane, Jane Peterson, and Carol Archbold. I remember our Saturday morning coffeehouse fondly.

The most substantial formal support for this project came to me in the form of a writing fellowship by the American Association of University Women. The fellowship offered much needed time and validation for the project.

The publication process with the University of Nebraska Press has been a smooth and rewarding process. I thank

Senior Acquisitions Editor Matthew Bokovoy for pursuing the project. Matthew has been both efficient and insightful. His broad knowledge on the issues involved in this project illuminated nuances of the writing that, I must admit, I often did not know were there. Thanks, also, to the anonymous reviewers for their time, effort, and feedback.

On a more personal note, I owe much to my husband, Keith, and sons, Cameron and Quinn. My parents, Marie and Walter Schrift, have always kept the faith in my writing. I offer a special nod to my mother for showing me my first Melungeon article. I thank my father for passing on his love of the water and teaching me how to swim. I actually mean this literally, though the metaphorical applies equally well. Thanks to the continued energy and support of the Pilkey family, who have closed ranks in a difficult year and reminded me how fortunate I am to be one of them. Finally, I owe much gratitude to my sisters, Tani Schrift and Stacy Beneville, who keep me both grounded and laughing.

INTRODUCTION

Race, Identity, and the Melungeon Legend

I entered the outdoor pavilion to see hundreds of people talking, laughing, and walking around. Clusters of people surrounded Brent Kennedy, who was shaking hands and posing for pictures with his newfound kin. A child who appeared to be twelve or so was singing on a makeshift stage. Donned in country attire, she had big brown eyes and long hair carefully shellacked around her head. According to the eight-by-ten glossy her mother handed me, her name was Shalacey Manderson, and she was singing "The Melungeon Song," written by her parents. I began to wander around as Shalacey sang the chorus.

> Once they stood with heads held high
> On fertile lands of green
> They must not be forgotten
> They're a part of you and me

I noticed a group of Turkish dancers off to the side preparing for a performance. They wore colorful scarves and layered clothing that billowed brilliantly against the stark Appalachian background. A couple of Turkish women huddled together, looking around the pavilion with interest. Shalacey continued her song:

> A people called Melungeons
> Their heritage unknown

Whose different way of life
Was all their own

Someone handed me a Turkish transcription of the song. I looked at a table stacked with memoirs and treatises on Melungeons. Other booths sold Native American jewelry and new age trinkets. Most of the people around me appeared to be middle-aged or retirement age. I passed a group of white-haired women talking excitedly about genealogy. One was knitting while she talked, sporting a round button attached to her shirt that read, "Maybe Melungeon?"

I was visiting Third Union, a four-day event sponsored by the Melungeon Heritage Association (MHA), packed with speakers, genealogical chats, and entertainment. It was May 2000, and I was in the early stages of a research project on the Melungeon legend. I came to Third Union hoping to talk to Melungeons. Save for the Melungeon books and buttons, Shalacey's song, and Kennedy's tireless affability, I might have thought I was in the wrong place at first. I had understood the Unions to be a meeting place for descendants of Melungeons. I did not necessarily go to the Union anticipating live versions of the Melungeon characters so vividly described in Appalachian legend — the exotic, dark-skinned rogues who rejected the outside world. However I also was not quite expecting to stumble into what appeared to be an elaborate family reunion of people who seemed so ordinary. In fact I remember thinking, throw in a few potato salads and drunken uncles and this could have been my own family reunion.

Like observers before me, I was familiar with the basics of the legendary tale: that Melungeons were a mysterious, multiethnic population who hibernated in the remote and rugged mountains in the farthest corner of northeast Tennessee. The alleged unknown origins of Melungeons drove the legend, resulting in myriad exotic-origin theories that involved everything from the Lost Colony to shipwrecked Turks. Since the late 1800s popular lore fancied Melungeons to be a wayward group of bandits who deeply resented the name given to them and were not to be trespassed upon. This mythical image also reflected a more romantic image of a mysterious and oppressed people who survived by their wits and integrity. Though nobody self-identified as Melungeon before the 1960s — and only a small number did then — by the 1990s Melungeonness had become a full-fledged phenomenon, resulting in a zealous virtual community on the Internet, the establishment of the MHA, and annual Melungeon Unions where a new movement of self-identified Melungeons gathered.

Unlike others interested in the Melungeon story, I am not interested in debating Melungeon origins. Instead my interests relate to the ways in which the Melungeon legend has been socially constructed vis-à-vis the media, and how that social construction evolved into a fervent movement of self-identified Melungeons in the 1990s. My interest in the social construction of Melungeon identity involves a number of interrelated questions: Who are the individuals today who claim a Melungeon identity, and by what processes do they establish and legitimate such claims? What does it mean to be Melungeon to those making the claim, and to what extent do these meanings represent and/or digress from the experiences of those labeled Melungeon historically? How have portrayals of Melungeons in popular writing changed over time, and to what extent have portrayals been internalized and/or resisted by individuals in Hancock County and those who self-identify as Melungeons? Finally, and on a broader level, how does the articulation of Melungeon identity resonate with larger racial and cultural politics in the contemporary United States?

It was at Third Union that I made my first attempt at interviews. I began with a boisterous man, Herbie, who was seated comfortably in the middle of the pavilion. He saw me passing with my notebook, leaned forward, and said, "You know who I am?" I did not but was thrilled to talk to someone. We began the interview with Herbie explaining who he was — in a nutshell, a "real" Melungeon, as well as one of the only real experts on Melungeons. I tried to redirect Herbie to talk about what he understood Melungeons to be. He laughed and told me that Melungeons were a cultural group who liked to have fun and said whatever they thought. As proof he told me how much he disliked my sandals.

The next person I spoke with was Larry Gibson. Larry was born and raised on Newman's Ridge and held the enviable status of being directly descended from Melungeons understood to originate on Newman's Ridge — an undeniable "Ridgemanite." At the Union Larry was leaning back on a chair under a shade tree, at some distance from the crowd. He was taking it all in with an amused expression. When he learned that I was an anthropologist, Larry was "tickled" and invited me to sit with him. He then goaded me with questions regarding why an anthropologist wanted to know anything about Melungeons. I liked him immediately.

While Larry and I were talking, an acquaintance of mine from the university passed. I knew she self-identified as Melungeon. She whispered conspiratorially to me that she would be sitting with the "Newman's Ridge clan." Larry leaned forward with feigned curiosity and asked, "Who are the Newman's Ridge clan?" She told him they were the first Melungeons and their clan leader was Jack Goins. Goins was known widely as one of the oldest core Melungeons, as well as one of the most determined and thorough Melungeon genealogists. He was also friends with

Larry. As my acquaintance walked away, Larry became even more animated. He kept repeating "clan leader" in his slow drawl, a big grin spreading across his face. After about an hour, I reluctantly moved on from my shady spot with Larry—though not before he got the chance to yell to Jack, "I heard from some lady here that you was the clan leader of the Melungeons." Larry was relentless as he teased Jack, laughing with abandon.

When I asked my next interviewee what it meant to be Melungeon, she told me not to worry about all the talk about Melungeons being from "here or there." "Melungeon only means Portuguese," she said. She told me that she had only recently discovered that she was Melungeon. She quickly followed with, "I have always thought of myself as white. I still think of myself as white—Melungeon white."

The final conversation I had that day was accidental. I was listening to a speaker and chose a spot on the outskirts with only one other woman there. She was one of the few still listening to the woman at the podium. We began to make small talk, and she introduced herself as Thelma. It was her first visit to a Union. She had only come because her mother had recently passed away; she felt like she could finally check it out without betraying her family. Although Thelma had moved outside of east Tennessee as an adult, she was born and raised in Hancock County; her mother grew up on Newman's Ridge. She had to leave the Union to go to work but agreed to meet with me at another time.

When I visited Thelma months later in her home, her husband joined us at the kitchen table. She spoke in front of him in a more censored way, and I got the impression that he was monitoring our talk. Having grown up in Hancock County, Thelma did not remember hearing people use the term Melungeon, but she remembered knowing about it as a young woman. She recalled one of her early arguments with her husband. He accused her of being stubborn, and she blurted out, "I guess that's just the Melungeon in me." They looked at each other with shock, laughed, and did not speak of it again. Her husband said that he knew Thelma was Melungeon when he married her, because her family was from "the ridge," but that they did not talk about it. He said that it was never a problem for him, making a point to say that there was "no nigger in a woodpile here." Thelma looked embarrassed and changed the topic to her interest in the Melungeon movement as an adult. When she had asked her mother about being Melungeon, her mother had reacted negatively. Thelma's mother told her that Melungeons in Hancock County had always had to hide who they were and that Thelma's interest in resurrecting family history would only put them back "under that rock." Thelma abided by her mother's wishes to not pursue her interests in Melungeons until her mother passed away. Third Union was her first foray into the new world of Melungeons. She was not critical of the event, but she had satisfied her curiosity and did not plan to return.

My introduction to Thelma and others at Third Union left me with a couple of strong impressions that shaped my research pursuit. The first was that issues of ethnicity, race, and identity were far more nuanced and complex than I, even as a cultural anthropologist, realized at the time. The second was that the real story about Melungeons no longer existed in the mysteries of the past but rested with the contemporary amalgam of Turkish dancers, knitting grandmothers, Ridgemanites, and shoe critics who gathered together as Melungeons in the present.

Melungeons: An Overview

According to C. S. Everett (1999), the term "Melungeon" most likely derived from the French *mélange*, or mixed people. The earliest reliable ethnographic sources understood Melungeons to be one of many southeastern tri-racial isolates that emerged from intermarriage among whites, blacks, and American Indians. By 1800 these isolates occupied Newman's Ridge, in an area that included much of east Tennessee and southwest Virginia and today lies in Hancock County, a poor and remote corner of northeast Tennessee. The most common family surnames associated with these early Melungeons include Bolins, Bunch, Collins, Gibson, Goins, and Mullins.

No evidence exists that anyone self-identified as Melungeon before the late 1960s; thus it is reasonable to suggest that the term was imposed by outsiders as a derogatory one. The earliest printed reference to the term can be found in the minutes from the Stony Creek Primitive Baptist Church in 1813. In the minutes one church member accused another of harboring "them Melungins" (cited in Winkler 2004, 55). This reference occurred at the same time that individuals with Melungeon surnames were either reprimanded or removed from the church. As Everett (1999) points out, the context in which the term was employed suggests that it served as a pejorative epithet. At the same time that Melungeons were banished from the church, they settled in larger numbers on Newman's Ridge. No tangible proof suggests that the settlement of Newman's Ridge was the result of any kind of coerced geographical retreat; Melungeons bought and owned the land they settled. Although the extent of discrimination faced by Melungeons is the topic of some debate (DeMarce 1996), it is reasonable to accept that, like other mixed-race groups, Melungeons faced varied forms of intolerance.

As Helen Rountree (1990) points out, from the 1830s on, the stage was set for conflict between multiracial groups in the Southeast and the dominant white society. While Native American tribes were forcibly removed to reservations at this time, many mixed, or fringe, groups in the Southeast stayed behind; due to their ethnic ambiguity, they were typically understood as marginal, and, there-fore, not real Indians (Rountree 1990). These non-reservation Indians, or tri-racial groups, were assumed to have some African descent and, most often, carried the label of "free persons of color."

The indeterminate lineage of these groups upset society's increasingly strict racial categories. Philosophies of racial purity were becoming entrenched in the nineteenth century, epitomized by the "one-drop rule" — a belief that any individual with even one drop of negro blood would be categorized as black. Growing concerns about racial purity were eventually formalized into law throughout the South, targeting negro and mixed-race populations. Virginia's laws of 1831 and 1832 were particularly stringent, down-grading the status of free negroes and Indians to that of slaves (Rountree 1990). Laws in North Carolina (1835) and Tennessee (1834) followed suit, enacting blood quantum legislation for Native Americans that disenfranchised individuals with any African descent.

In the wake of the disenfranchisement laws of the 1830s, mixed-race groups basically had two options: to assimilate (with blacks or lower-class whites) or to strive to become publically legitimate Native American tribes. For the dozens of mixed-race groups in the Southeast, the latter would be much more difficult than the former; as Karen Blu reasons, in the climate of the one-drop rule, "Indianness is easy to lose and blackness is easy to gain" (Blu 2001, 4). Groups who did aim for Indianness had to work within a system of racial classification imposed by white society.

One of the best-documented examples of a multiracial group who pursued formal recognition is the present-day Lumbee, a group of Indians in Robeson County, North Carolina.[1] In the wake of the 1835 North Carolina disenfranchisement law, the Indians of Robeson County adamantly rejected their classification as free negroes and, instead, fought for legal recognition as Indians. In the attempt to establish a tribal identity, Robeson County Indians had a couple of strikes against them, including the long-held assumptions of their partial African heritage and their relatively comfortable degree of assimilation into the white society around them. However by 1885 Robeson County Indians received state recognition as Croatan Indians, based on state legislator Hamilton McMillan's theory that Robeson County Indians provided refuge as well as marriage candidates for Europeans from the Lost Colony (Lowery 2010). This linkage to the Lost Colony authenticated Robeson County Indians by providing the necessary "historic aura" of the time. As Malinda Lowery describes it: "For most non-Indians at this time, being 'Indian' depended on what 'tribe' one descended from. Identifying a historic lineage was necessary in the minds of white North Carolinians, who desired assurance that these Indians were a distinct racial group and not in fact African Americans. An identification as Croatan provided not only a tribal name but also a noble heritage. Hidden behind the name 'Croatan' was a legend of white ancestry, white sacrifice, and white heroism" (Lowery 2010, 26).

As with the Lumbee, the blood quantum laws became inextricably linked with the ethnogenesis of a handful of southeastern Native American groups. In the process of becoming Indian, however, it became mandatory to deny blackness. In her work on the Powhatan and other Virginia tribal groups, Rountree (1990) explains that eschewing blackness not only enabled Native Americans to escape the negative ramifications of being black but, indeed, became a necessary criterion to prove one's true Indianness. With the abolition of slavery, Reconstruction, and the introduction of Jim Crow laws, it became ever more necessary for American Indians on the eastern seaboard to separate themselves from their mixed-race legacies and strategize a distinct group identity (Lowery 2010; Rountree 1990). Formally recognized American Indian groups tightened their tribal boundaries, inevitably excluding mixed-race individuals outside those illusory ethnic parameters. In her discussion of the evolution of the Lumbee in the Jim Crow South, Lowery (2010) points out that these exclusionary tactics mimicked the tenets of white supremacy at the time, despite the fact that they posed painful inconsistencies with Indian notions of kinship and family.

While Native American groups maintained vigil to both become and remain Indian, those mixed-race individuals for whom Indianness was not an option faced a similarly perilous environment. In response to this historical legacy of discrimination, claims to a partial Portuguese ancestry became necessary and expedient for many mixed-raced individuals, including the Melungeons (Everett 1999; Hashaw 2006; Price 1951). As many mixed-race people found themselves less Indian, this Portuguese escape valve became all the more critical. The idea of Portuguese heritage stands as a point of contention in discussions about and among Melungeon descendants. While theories of Portuguese and Mediterranean ancestry remain popular today, academics are quick to point out that it was quite common for historic mixed-race peoples to claim a Portuguese or Mediterranean identity to obfuscate black ancestry while explaining darker skin (DeMarce 1996; Everett 1999; Henige 1998).

While certain families with Melungeon surnames were legally established as white by this time and, thereby, less vulnerable to the laws of the 1830s, the stability of their whitened identities was negligible. With the dawn of the twentieth century, their status became increasingly threatened, owing primarily to a eugenics crusade against Virginia's "mongrels" or mixed Indians, catalyzed by W. A. Plecker, head of Virginia's Bureau of Vital Statistics in the early 1900s. A former physician and eugenics enthusiast, Plecker dedicated his career to unearthing and subjugating tri-racial people. Plecker's fixation on mixed-race groups was fortified by other eugenicists as well. One of his most notable allies was Dr. Arthur Estabrook who traveled through Virginia to conduct his own study of mixed communities. His resulting publication, *Mongrel Virginians* (Estabrook and McDougal, 1926), provided a compendium of gossip, innuendo, and his own unsubstantiated observations to argue for the degeneracy of mixed-race peoples.

The work of Estabrook, Plecker, and other popular eugenicists of the time contributed to Virginia's 1924 Racial Integrity Act, legislation that demanded stricter definitions of racial purity to prevent miscegenation. The law unleashed Plecker's crusade against mixed-race communities, including Melungeons, and he worked tirelessly to "correct" racial identities on birth certificates and redefine a history of census identifications. In a 1942 correspondence with Tennessee's state archivist, Ms. John Trotwood Moore, Plecker solicits evidence of Melungeons' racial lineage. Dissatisfied with conjecture regarding Melungeon claims to any Indian and Portuguese heritage provided by Moore, Plecker determines the formal fate of Melungeon classification in his response: "We have found after very laborious and painstaking study of records of various sorts that none of our Virginia people now claiming to be Indian are free from Negro admixture, and they are, therefore, according to our law classified as colored. In that class we include the melungeons of Tennessee" (cited in Winkler 2004).

One year later Plecker's work culminated in an ominous declaration to all Virginia county officials. With regard to Virginia's "mongrels," Plecker writes:

> Now that these people are playing up the advantages gained by being permitted to give "Indian" as the race of the child's parents on birth certificates, we see the great mistake made

in not stopping earlier the organized propagation of this racial falsehood. They have been using the advantage thus gained as an aid to intermarriage into the white race and to attend white schools and now for some time, they have been refusing to register with war draft boards as Negroes. . . . Some of these mongrels, finding that they have been able to sneak in their birth certificates unchallenged as Indians are now making a rush to register as white. . . . Those attempting this fraud should be warned that they are liable to a penalty of one year in the penitentiary. . . . Several clerks have likewise been actually granting them licenses to marry whites, or at least marry amongst themselves as Indian or white. The danger of this error always confronts the clerk who does not inquire carefully as to the residence of the woman when he does not have positive information. . . . Please report all known or suspicious cases to the Bureau of Vital Statistics, giving names, ages, parents and as much other information as possible. All certificates of these people showing "Indian" or "white" are now being rejected and returned to the physician or midwife, but local registrars hereafter must not permit them to pass their hands uncorrected or unchallenged and without a note of warning to us. One hundred and fifty thousand other mulattoes in Virginia are watching eagerly the attempt of their pseudo-Indian brethren, ready to follow in a rush when the first have made a break in the dike. (Plecker 1943, cited in Winkler 2004, 143)

As a result of Plecker's work, Melungeons were vulnerable along with multitudes of individuals who existed in the ill-fated space between black and white. While a handful of mixed-race groups rallied for formal Native American recognition, for most tri-racial peoples assimilation was the best option. It is important to reiterate that the concept of ethnogenesis does not apply to Melungeons historically. Unlike the Indians of Robeson County, or the Powhatan of Virginia, individuals did not self-identify as Melungeon until the mid-twentieth century. The net result of the eugenics onslaught against mixed-race individuals was the disappearance of many peoples with rich, historically significant ethnic legacies.

Paralleling this figurative disappearance was a physical one. With the industrialization of Appalachia beginning in the late 1800s, many mountain communities dissolved as individuals left their farms to find work in the mining, timber, and textile industries. Families moved from their rural farms to company towns that offered substandard housing, dangerous working conditions, and labor unrest that led to violence and death. By the early 1900s many of the industries that promised to secure Appalachia's financial prosperity folded, leaving Appalachian individuals and families impoverished and embittered (Drake 2001; Eller 1982).

By the time the nation was felled by the stock market crash in 1929, mountain families were already destitute, without the land and kinship ties that would allow even the most meager self-subsistence. The ensuing years of the Great Depression decimated Appalachia, with disease, hunger, and cold weather plaguing the area. Relief programs that began with the New Deal in 1933 bore a modest impact on Appalachia; however by 1936 close to half of its inhabitants survived on welfare, unable to sustain their families (Eller 1982).

The most prominent symbol of the New Deal policies in Appalachia was the establishment of the Tennessee Valley Authority (TVA). Proposed as an economic development initiative, the TVA promised flood control, agricultural support, and electricity to the Appalachian region. Despite the best intentions of the government, however, the TVA exacerbated the downward spiral of the Appalachian economy, primarily through its aggressive acquisition of land. Massive purchases of land by the TVA resulted in the displacement of thousands of mountain families. Hydroelectric facilities built by the TVA replaced prime farmlands, relocating families whose traditional way of life was being interrupted by modernization. Writing about the impact of the construction of the Norris Dam, Michael McDonald and John Muldowny characterize TVA's effect on families as a "disastrous wrenching away from familiar surroundings and a disruption of the sense of community established through generations" (McDonald and Muldowny 1982, 195). In his critique of the TVA, Ronald Eller (1982) quotes a letter written by a displaced farmer, William Wirt, in 1938. Describing the changed environment around him, Wirt writes:

> One day we were the happiest people on earth. But like the Indian we are slowly but surely being driven from the homes that we have learned to love, and down to the man we are not a friend of the Government for the simple reason that every move they have made has increased our poverty. . . . Now what are we going to do, move on and try to fit in where we do not belong or undertake to face the situation and gradually starve to death? In the little mountain churches where we once sat and listened to the preaching of the gospel with nothing to disturb us, we now hear the roar of machinery on the Sabbath day. After all I have come to believe that the real old mountaineer is a thing of the past and what will finally take our place, God only knows. (cited in Eller 1982, 242)

While many Appalachians like Wirt bemoaned the razing of the Appalachian landscape and culture, many others sought redemption in the northern factories catering to the World War II defense industry. This mass migration brought welcome economic opportunities that also came with more family separation and, for those who left, a similar sense of displacement. At this time, many individuals from core Melungeon families migrated north.

For Melungeons, migration held the distinct advantage of evading the full impact of Plecker's assault on multiethnic groups. Melungeon individuals who were suspect, by virtue of their genealogical and geographic associations, could escape the denotations of their last names by leaving the region. Often their identity choices changed with their move to the North; their opportunities to pass as white expanded, and, in general, the stigma associated with their names and histories was diluted as they joined a working force whose priority was production instead of ethnic gatekeeping. Reflecting on the migration of southeastern mestizo groups from the 1940s on, Brewton Berry (1963) writes: "If you ask them why they have migrated, they will speak of steady work, good wages, better living conditions. They will not admit that they also enjoy the privilege of attending integrated schools, making friends with whites, dating white boys and girls, even finding white wives or husbands. Yes, and if they choose to boast of their Indian blood, they can do so with pride, and not with the fear that it might evoke smirks and sneers" (Berry 1963, 173).

The industrialization of Appalachia inevitably generated a public nostalgia about a lost culture and vanishing people. According to David Whisnant (1983), it is this sentiment that was inextricably linked with the Appalachian cultural revival of bluegrass music, quilts, and crafts vis-à-vis missionary idealism. It is also within the shadow of this postindustrial wistfulness that the legend of the Melungeon gained more momentum in popular media. While Appalachians, in general, begin to stake a claim in their cultural presentation to outsiders, individuals from mixed-race backgrounds had no incentive to distinguish themselves from other Appalachians. As a self-identified group of people, Melungeons did not exist; yet, in the media they were consistently treated as one of Appalachia's best-kept secrets. Indeed as Appalachians became increasingly quaint and folksy in the public eye, the Melungeon legend served to perpetuate the idea of the exotic mountain other. With the increased access to Hancock County, Melungeon spottings by outsiders mushroomed, and public curiosity peaked. At the same time, many of those individuals who left their mixed-race legacies for the prosperous North—removed in place and time from their oppressive legacies—began to muse over who they were and where they came from. Though individuals would not actually begin to self-identify as Melungeon until the 1960s, the industrial fallout of migration, nostalgia, and increased outsider access formed the early alchemy of the Melungeon revitalization movement.

Melungeon Scholarship

A handful of academic writings in the 1940s and 1950s temper the media production of Melungeons with research-based descriptions of mixed-race peoples in the Southeast. William Gilbert (1946, 1948) conducted the most prolific early research on mixed-race peoples as part of his work with the Library of Congress. Gilbert defines the individuals in these racial islands as descendants from intermarriage among underclass whites, black slaves, and rebellious Indians. Though Gilbert offers only a brief sociological nod to these mixed-blood peoples, he provides valuable, comprehensive inventories of these surviving Indian groups of the Southeast. He estimates each group to include fifty thousand to one hundred thousand individuals across approximately twenty-eight states.

Another early researcher for the US Census, Calvin Beale, provides similar writing on tri-racial isolates (a term, according to Winkler, coined by Beale). As a worker for the 1950 census, Beale had a practical interest in studying mixed-race groups; it was his job to count and classify them. Like Gilbert, Beale provides less ethnographic information but produces a useful compendium of the varied people in the Southeast who existed as racial others (Beale 1957, 1972).

Offering slightly more ethnographic context than his contemporaries, a geographer named Edward Price conducted doctoral research on these same mixed-blood groups (Price 1951, 1953). Though Price recounts media folklore about Melungeons, he does so critically, noting the scant evidence of a distinct group of people who call themselves Melungeons. Price writes: "The core of reality within the legend is not easily discovered. There is no group of people who call themselves Melungeons or who would recognize themselves as thus separated from the rest of the country population. Non-Melungeons, however, are in general agreement as to who are Melungeons" (Price 1951, 258).

Though Price may well have discerned a larger community conceptualization of Melungeons, he does not provide evidence. In all of these early writings, a researcher named Brewton Berry attempts ethnographic detail on what he termed the "mestizos" of the South (Berry 1963). It is important to note that Berry's descriptions appear to rely wholly on his own perceptions of appearance versus any underlying reality; however Berry's work is interesting in that he travels to different mixed-race communities where he spends time observing and talking to people. His analysis of Melungeons and similar groups is consistent with his colleagues—that they represent tri-racial isolates once classified as "free persons of color." In describing Melungeons, he writes that "neither in their culture nor their economy are they distinguishable from other mountain folk. Among those bearing the telltale surnames are individuals of dark complexion and straight black hair, whose ancestry might well be Indian. But physical features of most of them suggest no other ancestry than white" (Berry 1963, 18).

Berry provides brief commentaries on the impressions of mixed-race people in the general community. Members of these communities instruct Berry on the specifics of detecting negro blood (varying from blue gums to misshapen feet). Others are more vague: "It just takes experience," or "You sort of know it instinctively" (Berry 1963, 43). At least one respondent admitted his ignorance about the mixed peoples in his community, suggesting to Berry: "I wish you would find out what they are and tell me. I want to know whether I ought to Mr. them or not when they come in here" (Berry 1963, 75). Berry concludes this about the perceptions of whites: "In short, the attitude of whites toward mestizos is a jumble of ignorance, indifference, prejudice, suspicion, pity, fear, bewilderment, and, above all, contradiction" (Berry 1963, 55). Berry reports that blacks in the community view mestizos striving to be Indian as misdirected. One respondent reasons: "They think they can solve their problem with feathers. . . . They ought to forget all that foolishness and join with us. We could do more for them than anybody else" (Berry 1963, 72).

In the 1970s and 1980s academics directed increased attention to Melungeons as individuals began to self-identify. The most valuable of these include a succinct ethnographic piece by Anthony Cavender (1981) and an unpublished dissertation by Sandra Keyes Ivey (1976). Cavender conducts interviews in Hancock County, resulting in one of the few field-based explorations of perceptions of Melungeons in the region where Melungeons are purported to exist. Cavender's work is significant in that he resists romanticizing Melungeons; instead he provides an ethnographic rendering of local understandings of Melungeonness in a specific time and place. He not only provides important primary source material, but he is the first, and one of the few, to critically reflect on Melungeonness as a social phenomenon. Ivey's (1976) work is similarly grounded in field-based research in Hancock County, and she also provides a wealth of primary source material through her interviews with individuals in the region. In addition Ivey explores representations of Melungeons in academic, folkloric, and journalistic writing up to the 1970s, when her dissertation was completed. Though she is less critical than Cavender, her work is unique in that she conducted field research in Hancock County during the staging of the Melungeon-themed outdoor drama, *Walk Toward the Sunset*.

Another piece of writing during this time period is Melanie Sovine's (1982) dissertation on what she terms the mythology of Melungeons. In her work Sovine delineates media themes on Melungeons through the 1970s; though she provides useful primary source material, she delivers the material in a telegraphic way that lacks analysis. Still, Sovine's work is distinctive in providing a long-overdue critical analysis of the media manufacture of Melungeon identity.

While many of these academic works remained unpublished and under the radar, Brent Kennedy's (1994a) self-proclaimed pseudo-academic writings on Melungeons in the mid-1990s shifted the focus once again to a more romantic Melungeon story. Though journalists from the late 1800s on toyed with the alleged exotic origins of Melungeons, Kennedy attempts to substantiate a Melungeon heritage that transcends the tri-racial framework. Taking account of early reports that Melungeons asserted a "Portyghee" identity, Kennedy proposes an ethnic admixture that includes early Mediterranean sailors, soldiers, and slaves, hailing primarily from Portuguese and Ottoman Turks. Kennedy lends particular weight to a Melungeon-Turkish connection and has expanded this notion into a well-established relationship with Turkish scholars and officials (Scolnick and Kennedy 2003). Though some scholars acknowledge potential Mediterranean admixture among Melungeons—noting the cases of Spanish and Portuguese explorers and settlers in early colonial America (DeMarce 1996; Everett 1999)—they also argue that Kennedy's preoccupation with Mediterranean origins has resulted in the invention of a race that offers an exoticism that obscures

African origins as well as sidesteps a more mundane northern European ancestry (DeMarce 1996; Henige 1998). From my perspective, both critiques are on point—and certainly are reflected in the ethnographic research in this book. I would argue, however, that, while Kennedy's work provides a framework for multiple racialized interpretations of identity, such interpretations are not at all implicit in Kennedy's assertions. In fact, to my knowledge Kennedy has never denied *any* ethnic ancestry—African, northern European or otherwise—but, instead, poses a Melungeon identity with ever-expanding parameters.

Some of the scholarship following Kennedy's writing offers a more judicious analysis of Melungeon history. Most notably Wayne Winkler's (2004) book on Melungeons represents the most comprehensive and balanced perspective to date. Written in journalistic form, Winkler's book is accessible and full of information wrought from a careful research ethic. The only drawback in Winkler's work is his tentative engagement with the new Melungeon movement. One senses that Winkler makes the choice to not pursue the post-Kennedy revitalization in depth; as Winkler is one of the more visible Melungeons himself, his choice is understandable and, overall, does not detract from an otherwise superb piece of work. Equally thorough, though more narrow in scope, Everett (1999) writes about Melungeons from a historical perspective. Responding to debates in the *Appalachian Quarterly* between Kennedy and his critics, Everett employs a fastidious methodology to reiterate the notion of historical Melungeons as a tri-racial isolate. He also provides a provocative commentary that contextualizes the new Melungeon movement within the "exotic origins craze." Finally, one of the newest writings on Melungeons by journalist Tim Hashaw (2006) contextualizes Melungeons within a history of mixed peoples in the United States, providing a refreshing and useful vantage point on the Melungeons.

A number of anthropological writings on Melungeons also appeared, beginning in the 1990s, including Anita Puckett's (2001) linguistic analysis and Patricia Beaver and Helen Lewis's (1998) reflection on resistance to multiculturalism in Appalachia. While Beaver and Lewis tend to be more sympathetic to the notion of Melungeons as a multicultural force in the region, Puckett invokes Bourdieu to suggest that individuals in the Melungeon movement find a distinction in being Melungeon that prioritizes a specific kind of ethnic whiteness. The Melungeon culture and history series at Mercer University Press has, likewise, produced an array of writing in recent years, most notably Katherine Vande Brake's (2001) book on Melungeon images in fiction and Jacob Podbers (2007) oral history work on the role of the Internet in sustaining a contemporary Melungeon community.

Defining Melungeons

The cacophony of Melungeon characters I met during the Melungeon Third Union—and the many more I met throughout my research process—presented a conundrum that became a fundamental component of doing research on Melungeons. Working on the topic of Melungeons felt like a project of chasing ghosts. When I became convinced that Melungeons were solely a figment of the public imagination, I would meet someone like Thelma who existed under the public radar with a story to tell. Other times I felt sure that if I just spent enough time scaling Hancock County, I would stumble across some kind of tangible experience among those identified, more often than not, as "real" Melungeons. I spent hours talking to people in this context and usually left more confused. Most of these individuals had no problems with their direct genealogical connections to core Melungeon families, yet they lived lives with no tangible memories of ever hearing the word Melungeon prior to the mid-1960s and no sense of being discriminated against or different beyond the fact that they were poor. Thus, in my research, interviews with individuals living in Melungeon-related areas resulted in an overwhelming lack of oral history evidence that being Melungeon related to any kind of experiential reality distinct from being Appalachian. Compounded by a dearth of convincing archival material, there is simply no evidence that Melungeons existed as a culturally bounded group of people.

This is not a particularly popular thing to say, given the media and public infatuation with the Melungeon story; yet the few ethnographers who have conducted research on Melungeons offer a similar interpretation. Reporting on his research in Hancock County, Cavender (1981) concludes with the following: "There is no consensus among Hancock Countians as to who or what is a Melungeon, but the identity persists because it functions as a symbolic marker of social class in the minds of a few Hancock Countians. Likewise, members of the country elite are involved in perpetuating Melungeon identity. They seek to keep the 'mysterious' connotations of the identity alive in an effort to capitalize on tourist interest, much to the dismay of many Hancock Countians who would like to forget about Melungeons forever" (Cavender 1981, 34).

Ivey (1976) reflects at some length about the contradiction inherent in trying to do field research on Melungeons. She writes: "To use the term Melungeon as if it refers to a group whose membership is defined by means of precise and generally accepted criteria within Hancock County is to reflect a contradiction which exists in that community. . . . In other words, county residents tend to speak of Melungeons as a group in a way that suggests that the group is defined by consensus. There may be considerable disagreement, however, as to whether a particular individual does or does not belong to the group. There are certain individuals, for example, who may be identified as Melungeons in certain contexts, but as non-Melungeons in others" (Ivey 1976, 15). Ivey's pursuit for answers to this contradiction within the community offers particularly valuable primary material that reinforces the notion that Melungeonness has long been, and continues to be, a social construction related primarily to social class. For example one of Ivey's respondents explained to her: "We don't sit around discussing it all the time, we just live with it. It's here and we don't talk about it much except when outsiders are here. Still, you do wonder about it, but not in relation to specific people" (Ivey 1976, 15).

Remarking on her choice to abandon fieldwork in Hancock County to shift focus to mythical representations of Melungeons, Sovine (1982) explains: "My first inclination was to design a fieldwork approach that would result in a more accurate portrayal of 'Melungeons' from the perspective of those to whom the term is applied. This inclination was based upon the assumption that an empirically designated and bounded Melungeon group exists which therefore can be identified for field research purposes. After careful review and to my present understanding, the assumption is wholly erroneous. It is nevertheless a persisting idea that a Melungeon population exists" (Sovine 1982, 8).

My goal in writing about the social construction of identity is not to deny the existence of or prove anything about core Melungeon families or individuals who currently claim Melungeon descent. Instead I find it more productive to conceptualize the Melungeon story as a regional legend that, similar to the structure of all legends, is a loosely structured narrative with an appealing story, a basis in actual belief, and a cultural message (Brunvand 1991). To write about a Melungeon legend points to an underlying theme in this work—that the only information that we can find out about a historical Melungeon identity is based almost exclusively on media and folkloric accounts. As addressed in the first part of this book, these accounts are social constructions that reproduce a story that has come to be accepted as truth. This legendary construction of Melungeons is central to the larger thrust of this book — that the contemporary Melungeon movement exists as a creative extension of the Melungeon legend from which individuals borrowed, perpetuated, and shaped to establish an identity that functions in meaningful ways in the twenty-first century.

Writing about contemporary Melungeonness requires certain important — if problematic — semantic distinctions. For example, those who embrace and celebrate a Melungeon identity today have become Melungeon in a context wholly different from the families in Newman's Ridge and elsewhere for whom the term itself was a misnomer. This irony results in an intriguing and perplexing scenario in which to pursue research on Melungeons. For the purposes of clarification, I use the term "Melungeon descendants" to refer to those individuals who self-identify as Melungeons today. As discussed in a later chapter, Melungeon descendant tends to be a preferred self-identifying term among individuals in the contemporary Melungeon movement.

It is important to note, however, that Melungeon descendants include a wide array of individuals with varied genealogical and geographical connections to those areas and individuals with surnames that reflect the tri-racial isolate of Melungeons historically. Thus, in parts of this book I opt for the phrase "core Melungeons" to refer to individuals born and/or raised in Melungeon areas with direct genealogical connections to historical Melungeons. I realize that these are imperfect categories, and they are not intended to presuppose that any particular group represents a more authentic version of Melungeonness. My interviews in core Melungeon areas certainly do not point to anything quintessentially Melungeon. Still, modest contrasts do emerge between groups that allow insight into a community of people whose reference point for discussing Melungeons is related to a specific sense of time and place. To ignore these differences assumes a false homogeneity and misses the nuances of the identity politics that are central to Melungeonness today.

The Racialization of Identity

My interests in the social construction of Melungeon identity via the media and the contemporary Melungeon movement relates to a broader literature on *racialization*, defined as the process by which racial identity and meaning is created (Omi and Winant 2004). Ethnic claims represent a significant extension of racialization in that they draw from a legacy of representation to adopt and enact identity narratives. Thus the racialization of identity becomes *performative*, whereby individuals selectively create identities, imbue them with meaning, and employ them in their everyday lives (Waters 1990). While individuals choose to stake identity claims for a range of idiosyncratic reasons, cues for when and how to construct and reproduce that identity are readily available through larger historical processes and social movements. For example the Melungeon revitalization is one of many examples of what Matthew Jacobson (2006) refers to as a post–Civil Rights "ethnic reverie." This reverie points to the escalation of white ethnicity as response to the new language of ethnic pride that emerged in the 1960s with the Civil Rights movement. According to several critics one legacy of the Civil Rights movement was a white identity crisis in which whites came to be linked with oppression and a vacuous culture (Jacobson 2006; Omi and Winant 2004). On one hand, ethnicity in general came to represent a premodern haven of authenticity distinct from industrialism, materialism, and commodification. In addition whites wanted to remove themselves from a history of domination. According to Jacobson (2006) the resulting "roots craze" involved genealogical searches among whites aimed to resurrect their ethnic ancestry.

Mary Waters (1990) addresses all of these issues in her extensive ethnographic work on the ways in which white individuals choose and understand different ethnic identities in the contemporary United States. Addressing the symbolic nature of such identities, she reveals the flexibility and flux with which individuals invent and drop self-identifications, as well as the elements of identity deemed preferable. According to Waters (1990) individuals base their choices on how they perceive the standing of various ethnic groups, with a tendency to opt for the more ethnic European ancestries, such as Polish, Irish, and Italian. These eastern and southern European identities hold the dual appeal of being not quite white (Brodkin 1998) while also being alchemized in the United States as more white than black (Jacobson 1998).

Waters explains the appeal of symbolic ethnicity as a mechanism to gain a sense of rootedness while still feeling distinctive. Waters also elaborates on the ways in which this white ethnic revival is problematic in terms of larger racial politics. She points out that nonwhite ethnic groups are typically not afforded the same leeway in identity choice; thus symbolic ethnicity becomes another component of white privilege. Waters persuasively argues that one of the end results of white ethnicity is the notion that all ancestries are equal. For example her respondents focus on stories of discrimination and adversity when speaking about their ethnic ancestors immigrating to the United States. Many respondents parallel their ancestors' toil with the oppression of nonwhite ethnic groups, concluding that all groups should be able to succeed, with the right degree of initiative. Reflecting on her respondents' ideas about ethnic discrimination, Waters states, "If the Irish had to sit at the back of the bus sometimes in the past, and now being Irish just means having fun at funerals, then there is hope for all groups facing discrimination now" (Waters 1990, 163).

Research by Michael Omi and Howard Winant (2004) and Jacobson (2006) reiterates the notion that issues of racism recede from the forefront as ethnic whites frame their newfound identities in relation to all other ethnic groups. The bootstrap mythology so replete in the immigrant story enables an analogous claim to historical suffering that excuses ethnic whites from historical tyrannies. At the same time it makes those tyrannies relative to any other hardship.

Given the disillusionment with whiteness about which these authors write, it is, perhaps, not surprising that seven million Americans chose the new multiracial option on the 2000 Census (Hartigan 2005). A large majority of these new white ethnics resort to a familiar refrain—claims to a white and Native American identity. In her critical analysis of the appropriation of Native American identity among whites, Eva Marie Garroutte (2003) describes this kind of ethnic switching or ethnic fraud as an access card to the cultural capital associated with Native American spirituality and identity. More recently Circe Sturm (2007) explores these issues of what she terms "racial shifting," with primary focus on whites becoming Native American in the last decade. Sturm relates these shifts to the historical phenomenon of racial passing, whereby nonwhite individuals aspired to a social and legal whitening to ascend in status (Burma 1946; Harper 1998; Henschel 1971). Like Garroutte, Sturm argues that racial shifting relates less to perceptions of financial benefits and more to intangible benefits, such as a perceived spiritualism associated with Native American culture. In most cases becoming Indian is fraught with cultural politics steeped in issues of cultural appropriation and racial essentialism.[2]

In the case of Melungeons the context is similar to that posed for all individuals shifting to a white ethnic identity, be it from Native American or Italian American. In this book I argue that the contemporary revitalization of Melungeon identity borrows from the past to create a new white ethnicity that capitalizes on the cache of the cultural exotic while underplaying stigmatized aspects of heritage. I trace the ways in which individuals employ genealogy, blood metaphors, narratives of oppression, and physiological traits as they become Melungeon. In this way the process of becoming Melungeon reflects a kind of racial passing from a collectively imagined whiteness to a more desirable non-white, or, perhaps, off-white, otherness. This idea of otherness involves ideas about whiteness, blackness, and Indianness that purport to imagine race in new (but no less essentialized) ways in the twenty-first century. This "imaginary," or ways to conceptualize identity, concerns itself with an attempt to not just pass between races, but to surpass race altogether.

Researching Melungeons

Drawing from fieldwork with working class whites in Detroit, Hartigan (1999) crafts a particularly useful framework for ethnographic pursuits on the racialization of identity:

> In order to think differently about race we need to pay attention to the local settings in which racial identities are actually articulated, reproduced, and contested, resisting the urge to draw abstract conclusions about whiteness and blackness. . . . The assertion that race is culturally constructed will remain a stunted concept unless it is linked to a heightened attention to the ways people actually construct meaningful lives in relation to race. (Hartigan 1999, 4)

My research process on Melungeons includes the two broad components of ethnographic and archival data collection. The majority of my data collection took place from October 1999 to May 2002 while I was living and working in Tennessee. After moving to Wisconsin, then back to Tennessee, I conducted additional follow-up interviews and archival research from August 2002 to the present. In terms of ethnographic work, I relied on semi-structured interviews, an in-depth questionnaire, oral histories, and participant-observation. I attended the Third, Fourth, and Fifth Melungeon Unions, each of which lasted approximately three days. I also participated in a gathering at Newman's Ridge in Hancock County, Tennessee, and observed a formal hearing in Nashville, Tennessee, focused on state recognition for Melungeons. The Newman's Ridge and Union gatherings involved observation of dozens of presentations and performances, including the opportunity to join several family chat sessions where a group of individuals with common surnames gathered to discuss their heritage. I conducted semi-structured interviews with Union participants, ranging from thirty minutes to one hour in length. I created and distributed a lengthy questionnaire (see Appendix 1) to participants at Melungeon Unions and received seventy-six completed questionnaires. Questionnaires solicited basic demographic information, as well as qualitative responses to over forty questions related to Melungeon identity. Questions concerned perceptions of race in general as well as specific ethnic groups. Respondents answered questions on Melungeon self-identification and the meanings they associated with Melungeon identity.[3]

I also completed multiple trips to Hancock County, Tennessee, and Wise, Scott, and Lee Counties in Virginia to conduct life history interviews with individuals who grew up on Newman's Ridge and were directly descended from core Melungeon populations. These individuals were typically born and raised in Hancock County, as well as in Lee, Scott, and Wise Counties. They typically possessed one of the original Melungeon surnames and without exception have established direct descent from historical Melungeon families. Some of these individuals have become visible public figures in the Melungeon movement; others have lingered on the sidelines or showed little awareness of or interest in Melungeons. All of the individuals were at least in their mid-fifties, and most were in their seventies or older. The overwhelming majority grew up on Newman's Ridge. Interviews ranged from one to three hours in length and involved multiple visits with approximately fifteen individuals. In Hancock County I also visited Melungeon sites on Newman's Ridge, including Mahala Mullins cabin and the refurbished church and school of the Vardy Historical Society. The church and school served as a missionary outpost for the Vardy community that was comprised primarily of core Melungeon families. Finally, I conducted extensive archival research at several special collections on Appalachia. I gathered hundreds of regional and national newspaper and magazine articles on Melungeons, dating from the late 1800s to the present.[4]

Chapter Overview

This book contains two main foci related to the social construction of Melungeons: 1) media portrayals; and 2) perceptions of identity among Melungeon descendants and core Melungeons. The initial focus of the book explores media representations of Melungeons from 1880 to the present. In chapter one I examine the earliest media articles on Melungeons, beginning in the late 1800s, to critically examine the foundation of the Melungeon narrative. Chapter two is closely related, providing textual analysis of media representations over the last two hundred years. Specifically I examine ways in which the media reproduce the Melungeon legend through an inspired repetition of fanciful tropes based primarily on borrowed information rather than firsthand experience. Chapter three discusses the outdoor drama on Melungeons, *Walk Toward the Sunset*, held in Hancock County in the late 1960s and early 1970s. The drama represents a substantial turning point in the Melungeon legend as it publically introduces the term "Melungeon" for the first time in Hancock County and stages the Melungeon story in the local community. I begin by discussing the formation, promotion, and community reception of the Melungeon drama, drawing from Hancock County newspaper articles and interviews. I also examine the regional and national publicity associated with the play, including the popular, but short-lived, "Melungeon tours."

Chapters four and five deal with the social construction of Melungeon identity, presenting ethnographic research on the contemporary Melungeon movement. Chapter four addresses what it means to be Melungeon from the perspective of those who encounter and claim the identity in their adult lives. My intent is to outline the contemporary Melungeon imaginary by reporting on how Melungeon descendants conceptualize their newfound identity and their process of becoming Melungeon. I also suggest ways in which individuals aim to secure their Melungeon identity through genealogical evidence, narratives of oppression, and physical characteristics and illnesses popularly understood to be Melungeon. Finally I focus on the personal and cultural meanings intertwined with becoming Melungeon.

In chapter five I focus on the ways in which Melungeon identities become racialized in the contemporary United States. More specifically I address ways in which self-identified Melungeons understand race on a general level, as well as how they internalize and resist understandings of blackness, whiteness, and Indianness. I then consider the additional category of Mediterraneanity in contemporary Melungeon identity-making.

Chapter six continues the theme of contemporary Melungeonness with a shift in focus from the larger movement of Melungeon descendants to core Melungeon individuals. I draw from fieldwork and oral history interviews to discuss the perceptions among core Melungeons of the contemporary Melungeon movement and how their experiences with and meanings of Melungeonness differ from Melungeon descendants. I also include an excerpt from an in-depth interview with Brent Kennedy. Kennedy reflects on his own experience in learning that he was Melungeon and on his place in the larger movement. Kennedy also engages questions related to the cultural and racial politics that form the premise of this book.

CHAPTER ONE

Inventing the Melungeons

As many mixed-race individuals struggled to pass—and disappear—into white society, their mythical shadow surfaced in popular writing. The mythical Melungeon, or the image that emerged from the media, materialized in a time period that involved a trio of historical forces. These included a national literary phase of local color writing, the pursuit of missionary agendas in the Appalachia region, and the industrialization of Appalachia.

Appalachia as a distinct region became prominent in the national imagination primarily through local color writers who returned from brief visits to the region with lively depictions of a "strange land and peculiar people."[1] The local color school was a national post–Civil War phenomenon that aimed to illustrate the heterogeneity of the nation's minority pockets. Local color writing served to accentuate—without threatening—the national rhetoric of a unified nation. Aimed primarily toward middle class, urban, literate Northerners, local color writing accessorized the new national theme of homogeneity with quaint and lively footnotes (Drake 2001, 123; Shapiro 1978, 3). The local color school was not specific to the Appalachia region; however, Appalachia proved fertile ground for the colorful narratives of the era. The effect of local color writing in Appalachia, and elsewhere, was to create images of an exotic otherness. In

Appalachia this image evolved into what Anthony Harkins (2004, 29) terms the "dualistic icon of the hillbilly-mountaineer." According to Harkins, the early hillbilly characterizations introduced a quirky and carefree simpleton, living in poverty without knowledge of or interest in modernity. However this image changed with the push toward industrialization, and the mountaineer emerged as a menace to civilization (Harkins 2004). These coexisting images presented a complex picture with the cumulative effect of romanticizing a preindustrial past while simultaneously celebrating and, inevitably, rationalizing the industrial future.

As missionary pursuits proliferated in the mountains, missionaries borrowed from and elaborated on the Appalachian narrative (Shapiro 1978). The uplift literature of the missionaries retold stories of the simple mountaineer, yet, increasingly, invoked hints of a necessary change among the unschooled and unchurched mountain people. From the vantage point of missionaries, Appalachia became less an amusement and more of a challenge. Thus the missionary agenda aligned naturally with the modernization of Appalachia. Economic advancement became part of the logic of missionary benevolence, and by the turn of the century the invention of Appalachian need had successfully resulted in the introduction of roads and railways and the expansion of the mining industries (Shapiro 1978). It is within this context that the first popular writings on Melungeons appear.

In this chapter I begin a discussion of media representations of Melungeons from the late 1800s to the present. In particular, I focus on the early, seminal articles that introduced Melungeons to the popular public. The cultural significance of these early writings cannot be underestimated, as they are integral in establishing the foundation of the Melungeon legend. These are the sources through which individuals today untangle Melungeon histories and identities; most, if not all, popular writings that follow either retell or refer to these early writings as original knowledge or lore. Yet, early media representations of Melungeons raise profound issues of ethnographic legitimacy. These early authors offer little to no context and often add fantastical details, resulting in a media-constructed version of identity that lacks any credibility.

In the Beginning

An article in the nineteenth-century magazine *Littell's Living Age* provides an appropriate starting point to discuss popular writing on Melungeons. As pointed out by C. S. Everett (1999), this article represents the first textual use of "Melungeon" to refer specifically to a mixed-race population in Hancock County, Tennessee. The article identifies the writer only as an "intelligent and sprightly correspondent, sojourning at present in one of the seldom-visited nooks hid away in our mountains" (The Melungeons 1849, 618). The original source of the piece is unknown, though Everett (1999) states that it was reprinted first in the *Knoxville Register* in 1848.

The *Littell's* article becomes immediately suspect as the author characterizes Melungeon culture. Although the author acknowledges traveling to Hancock County with a local doctor and visiting "old Vardy," the piece reads more as a folksy adventure tale than an ethnographic account (although readers are assured that "this is no traveler's story"). The author claims that the Melungeons formed a delightful utopia that prioritized drinking and debauchery over marriage and religion. As illustration, the writer relays a suspiciously colorful adventure with the Melungeons:

> We arrived at Vardy's in time for our supper, and, that dispatched, we went to the spring, where were assembled several rude log huts, and a small sprinkling of "the natives," together with a fiddle and other preparations for a dance. Shoes,

stockings, and coats were unknown luxuries among them—at least we saw them not. The dance was engaged in with right heart good will, and would have put to the blush the tame step-pings of our beaux. Among the participants was a very tall, raw-boned damsel, with her two garments fluttering readi-ly in the amorous night breeze, whose black eyes were lit up with an unusual fire from repeated visits to the nearest hut, behind the door of which was placed an open-mouthed stone jar of new-made corn whiskey, and in which was a gourd, with a "deuce a bit" of sugar at all, and no water nearer than the spring. Nearest her on the right was a lank, lantern-jawed, high-cheeked, long-legged fellow, who seemed similarly ele-vated. Now these two, Jord Bilson (that was he) and Syl Var-min (that was she) were destined to afford the amusement of the evening; for Jord, in cutting the pigeon-wing, chanced to light from one of his aerial flights right upon the ponder-ous pedal appendage of Syl, a compliment which this amiable lady seemed in no way disposed to accept kindly.

"Jord Bilson," said the tender Syl, "I'll thank you to keep your darned hoofs off my feet."

"Oh, Jord's feet are so tarnal big he can't manage 'em all by hisself," suggested some pacificator near by.

"He'll have to keep 'em off me," suggested Syl, "or I'll short-en 'em for him."

"Now look ye here, Syl Varmin," answered Jord, somewhat nettled at both remarks, "I didn't go to tread on your feet, but I don't want you to be cutting up any rusties about. You're nothing but a cross-grained critter, anyhow."

"And you're a darned Melungen."

"Well, if I am, I ain't nigger-Melungen, anyhow—I'm In-dian-Melungen, and that's more 'an you is."

The writer further describes a "grand me lee" involving the entire group, during which Syl Varmin exacts revenge. According to the author, everyone reconciles and refills the

Inventing the Melungeons

alcohol in the morning. The author promises to regale his readers with more "amusing incidents," although a sequel to the *Littell's* article never materialized.

As ethnographic source, this sketch is problematic in several ways. Since the author is unknown, no background exists for the story. Readers have no idea who visited Hancock County, when, for how long, and under what circumstances. The alleged remoteness and insular nature of the Melungeon community — by the author's own admission — suggests an environment in which it seems unlikely, at best, that an outsider would be welcomed into the middle of a drunken Melungeon jamboree-cum-brawl. It seems equally unlikely that individuals would have identified themselves — or their combative associates — as Melungeons, particularly in such light-hearted ways, given that the term is understood to have been a negative racial epithet. The story is also rife with stereotypes of Appalachians as barefoot, feuding moonshiners, and the droll delivery is typical of antebellum humor pieces of the time (Ivey 1976).

Another commonly referenced early source on Melungeons involves a brief commentary by Swan Burnett, published in the *American Anthropologist* in 1889. Burnett was not an anthropologist and, by his own admission, was not basing his commentary on field research: "It was not, however, until I had left east Tennessee and become interested in anthropology . . . that the peculiarities of this people came to have any real significance for me, and I was then too far away to investigate the matter personally to the extent I desired. I have, however, for several years past pursued my inquiries as best I could through various parties living in the country and visiting it, but with no very pronounced success"(Burnett 1889). Despite Burnett's disclaimer, his commentary is published in a prominent academic journal and written in an ethnographic voice. He describes the Melungeons: "They are dark but of a different hue to the ordinary mulatto, with either straight or wavy hair, and some have cheek bones almost as high as the Indians. The men are usually straight, large and fine looking, while one old woman I saw was sufficiently haglike to have sat for the original Meg Merriles."

Wayne Winkler (2004) suggests that Burnett's article may well have been the catalyst for a female Nashville reporter named Will Allen Dromgoole, whose infamous writings resulted in the most significant momentum to the popular Melungeon narrative. Dromgoole's articles were sensationalistic and ethnocentric, producing a national template for future media coverage on Melungeons. The significance of Dromgoole's work rests with the fact that she visited Hancock County and talked to people who lived there. This attempt at cultural immersion imbued her work with the illusion of an ethnographic authority that subsequent journalists rarely questioned.

What is interesting in Dromgoole's writing is that little actual evidence exists that the people she talked to or interacted with identified as, or were identified by others, as Melungeons. The great irony of her work (and most early writing on Melungeons) is that she did not and, presumably, dared not use the term "Melungeon," as it was regarded as an insult. Although Dromgoole makes reference to Melungeons in a way that suggests she uncovered the mysteries of their culture, she offers little detail beyond impressionistic assumptions. The exaggerated and inflammatory nature of her depictions reveals less about Melungeons and more about her attempt to establish the legitimacy of being in a strange and different place with strange and different people. Her labored account of finding the Melungeons in the wilds of southern Appalachia is telling:

> Away up in an extreme corner of Tennessee I found them—them or it, for what I found is a remnant of a lost or forgotten race,

Inventing the Melungeons

huddled together in a sterile and isolated strip of land in one of the most inaccessible quarters of Tennessee. When I started out upon my hunt for the Malungeons various opinions and vague whispers were afloat concerning my sanity. My friends were too kind to do more than shake their heads and declare they never heard of such a people. But the less intimate of my acquaintances coolly informed me that I was "going on a wild-goose chase" and were quite willing to "bet their ears" I would never get nearer a Malungeon than at that moment. One dear old lady with more faith in the existence of the Malungeons than in my ability to cope with them begged me to insure my life before starting and to carry a loaded pistol. Another, not so dear and not so precautious, informed me that she "didn't believe in women gadding about the country alone, nohow." Still, I went, I saw and I shall conquer. (Dromgoole 1890a)

Dromgoole elaborates on her pilgrimage with assurances that her only agenda is a martyred ambition to seek truth: "Just here let me say if any one supposes I made the trip for the fun it might afford, he is mistaken. If any one supposes it was prompted by a spirit of adventure, or a love for the wild and untried, he is grievously in error. I have never experienced more difficulty in traveling, suffered more inconvenience, discomfort, bodily fatigue, and real dread of danger. It required almost superhuman effort to carry me on, and more than once, or a dozen times, was I tempted to give up" (Dromgoole 1890a).

Once she establishes that she was there, Dromgoole resorts to other tactics to make clear that she was in no typical Appalachian community. One of her first descriptions of a church gathering provides a stark portrait of the gross immorality of miscegenation:

I went one day to preaching on Big Sycamore, where the people are more mixed than on their native mountains. I found here all colors—white women with white children and white husbands, Malungeon women with brown babies and white babies, and one, a young copper-colored woman with black eyes and straight Indian locks, had three black babies, negroes, at her heels and a third [sic] at her breast. She was not a negro. Her skin was red, a kind of reddish-yellow as easily distinguishable from a mulatto as the white man from the negro. I saw an old colored man, black as the oft-quoted aces of spades, whose wife is a white woman. (Dromgoole 1890a)

Amidst this heyday of racial integration, Dromgoole attempts to distinguish pure Melungeons as individuals who bear a physical presence similar to Native Americans: "They are certainly very Indian-like in appearance. The men are tall, straight, clean-shaven, with small, sharp eyes, hooked noses and high cheek bones. They wear their hair long, a great many of them, and evidently enjoy their resemblance to the red man." Despite Dromgoole's repeated references to a Native American physicality, she tends to digress with odd commentaries on the ugliness of Melungeon women. For example she notes that the women are "small, graceful, dark and ugly." She seems to find favor only with the women's merry laugh and "small and well shaped" feet (Dromgoole 1890a).

In general, it is difficult to fully accept Dromgoole's physical depictions of the people with whom she visited, as her theatrical narrative often borders on the hysterical. During one visit, for example, she describes the entrance of a mother (or "Mai" as Dromgoole transcribes the dialect): "Mai came, and the saints and hobgoblins! The witch of Endor calling dead Saul from sepulchral darkness would have calked her ears and fled forever at the sight of this living, breathing Malungeon witch. Shakespeare would have shrieked in agony and chucked his own weird sisters where neither 'thunder, lighting nor rain' would ever have found them more. Even poor tipsy, turvy Tam O'Shanter would have drawn up his gray mare and forgotten to fly before this, mightier than Meg Merrilles herself" (Dromgoole 1890a).

Of particular interest in Dromgoole's portrayal of Mai is her allusion to Meg Merrilles, the very same reference made by Burnett one year earlier. It is unlikely that this is coincidental; Dromgoole probably borrowed from Burnett without acknowledging him. This does not, of course, invalidate Dromgoole's work, in and of itself, as writers of the time operated under entirely different codes of conduct in terms of publication. The reference does, however, signal Dromgoole's preference for melodramatic innovation over straightforward description.

In addition to describing physical appearances, Dromgoole spends a great deal of time recounting her perception of Melungeon lifestyles. Perhaps even more so than with physical descriptions, Dromgoole's assessment of Melungeon cultural traits ranges from the ethnocentric to the absurd. She describes the Melungeons as lazy, immoral, illiterate, filthy, violent, superstitious, defiant, cowardly, mysterious, and primitive. Although Dromgoole's descriptions are not far removed from other ethnocentric versions of Appalachians, she repeatedly attempts to make the case that the characteristics she describes are, indeed, proof that she is among a distinct group of people: "They are totally unlike the native Tennessee mountaineer, unlike him in every way. The mountaineer is liberal, trustful and open. The Malungeon wants pay (not much, but something) for the slightest favor. He is curious and suspicious and given to lying and stealing, things unknown among the native mountaineers" (Dromgoole 1890b).

Dromgoole continues to contrast the Melungeon with the typical Appalachian: "I paid fifteen cents for my dinner. A mountaineer would have knocked you down had you offered money for dinner under such circumstances. Bah! The Malungeon is no more a mountaineer than am I, born in the heart of the old Volunteer state" (Dromgoole 1890b). Dromgoole's resentment of her host's request for compensation — and the obvious categorization of her as outsider — fuels her malicious distinction between Melungeon and mountaineer:

> They are not at all like the Tennessee mountaineer either in appearance or characteristics. The mountaineer, however poor, is clean — cleanliness itself. He is honest. . . . he is generous, trustful, until once betrayed, truthful, brave, and possessing many of the noblest and keenest sensibilities. The Malungeons are filthy, their home is filthy. They are rogues, natural, "born rogues," close, suspicious, inhospitable, untruthful, coward-ly, and to use their own word, "sneaky." They are exceedingly inquisitive too, and will trail a visitor to the Ridge for miles, through seemingly impenetrable jungles, to discover, if may be, the object of his visit. They expect remuneration for the slightest service. The mountaineer's door stands open, or at most the string of the latch dangles upon the "outside." He takes you for what you seem until you shall prove yourself otherwise. (Dromgoole 1891)

Further impugning the Melungeon character, Dromgoole promises evidence that she does not divulge of the hostile and inhospitable nature of the Melungeon: "They are an unforgiving people, although, unlike the sensitive moun-taineer, they are slow to detect an insult, and expect to be spit upon. But injury to life or property they never forgive. Several odd and pathetic instances of the Malungeon hate came under my observation while among them, but they would cover too much space in telling" (Dromgoole 1891).

Dromgoole's mean-spirited depictions are particularly dubious in the context of what appears to be her problem-atic entrée into the community. She does not address, in any of her writings, how she made contact with the com-munity, how long she stayed, what she did while there, or what kinds of questions she asked. The almost total lack of a context from which she observes and writes is suspicious at best. The context that she does provide suggests a jaunt into the area that involved sporadic encounters with people with whom her interactions appear limited. It is clear from her writing that she did not feel welcome and experienced a great deal of discomfort. Her obsessive references to the stingy character of Melungeons imply that the community perceived her as an outsider. She begins the description of her journey with a desire for acceptance: "I went . . . determined to be one of them, so I wore a suit as nearly like their own as I could get it" (Dromgoole 1890a). Although one can only imagine Dromgoole's version of said suit, she did not blend as she might have hoped: "They wondered very much concerning my appearance among them" (Dromgoole 1890a). Dromgoole elaborates on her hosts' curiosity as she describes her trials in finding room and board:

And let me say, I have never drawn a good easy breath since I landed and found a dozen pairs of little black Indian eyes turned upon me. Always they are at the cracks, the chimney corner, "window hole," the door, peeping through the chinquapin and wahoo bushes, until I feel as if forty thousand spies were watching my movements. I had not dared to take out a pencil for three days, except last Monday night after I went to bed. I tried to write a letter in the dark, by a streak of light which fell through a chink in the door. But the next morning, when my hostess—a little snap-eyed, red-brown squaw—flung open my door (the room had but one, and she had removed the fastening, a wooden button, the night before) and sung out: "You, Joe!—time you's up out'n ther," and a little, limp, sleepy-looking Indian crawled out from a pallet of rags in the corner. I felt pretty sure the boy had been there to watch me, and so didn't try that kind of writing again. They are exceedingly suspicious and are as curious about me as can be. (Dromgoole 1890a)

Dromgoole further reveals that she doesn't disabuse her hosts of the assumption that she is traveling to the mountain springs for her health, yet she complains: "Still, they suspect me, and they come in droves to see me. Seven little brown women, with bare feet and corncob pipes, sat on the doorstep yesterday to see me go out." When Dromgoole attempts to engage them in conversation by telling them her name and age, the women respond by advising her that if she wasn't married yet, "it wair time." Dromgoole then appears to make a modest breakthrough as "one grizzle face old squaw kindly offered me a 'pull at her pipe'" (Dromgoole 1890a).

Despite Dromgoole's difficulties in the field, the very fact that she attempted field research validated her often-preposterous impressions as genuine knowledge. Unlike the author of the *Littell's* article, Dromgoole appears to have visited Hancock County and interacted with people. However it is not clear that she actually visited Melungeons, and, given her obvious limitations in interactions with the people she describes, accepting even the smallest details she offers as valid requires some suspension of belief. In the wave of popular writings that followed Dromgoole's articles, few writers claim firsthand experience with Melungeons or Hancock County. Instead they reproduce Dromgoole's writing, more often than not without citation and, in many cases, with Dromgoole's precise wording.

The next written account that assumed an authority equivalent to Dromgoole's — and became known to a broader public — is a 1914 memoir by Judge Lewis Shepherd. Shepherd's reminiscence on the "Celebrated Melungeon Case" of 1872 serves as an oft-cited original source on the existence and heritage of Melungeons. In his writing, Shepherd describes a case involving the marriage of a Melungeon woman to a wealthy Virginia farmer. Shortly after birthing a daughter, the woman died, leaving her husband to go violently insane with grief. The daughter was removed from the area under the care of her Aunt Betsy, who had instructions to stay away. Fifteen years later, relatives of the mentally ill farmer sued to claim his estate. Commissioned by a friend of Aunt Betsy, Shepherd fought the suit by producing the farmer's sole heir, his daughter. In response the litigants argued that the daughter was illegitimate, invoking her dead mother's alleged negro background. Testimony accused the mother's entire family of having black blood, evidenced by their kinky hair. With a lock of the daughter's straight, coal-black hair attached to a deposition, Shepherd argued a romantic Carthaginian origin for the girl and her Melungeon heritage. Shepherd won the case, establishing both an important legal precedent for Melungeons denying African ancestry and providing a public building block for a theory of exotic Melungeon origins.

In most ways Shepherd's writing offers an original filter to view Melungeons; yet, when he strays from the discussion of his case to a more fanciful overview of the Melungeons, his meanderings hint at an imaginative elaboration of Dromgoole. For example he argues that in the case of mating between a white man and Melungeon woman, their children will never blend in color: "Some of them will be white like the father, and some of them dark like the mother. Sometimes the women bear twins by a white sire, and one will be white and the other one dark. The spectacle has often been seen of a mother suckling twin babies at each of her breasts, one white and the other dark. This is not true of a cross between a white man and a negro woman. A mulatto is always half white and half black, and an octoroon can hardly be told from a pure Caucasian, the negro blood being so completely bred out."

Shepherd's description directly echoes Dromgoole's scene in the churchyard, with the provocative twist of a mother's white and dark babies simultaneously suckling at her breasts. Despite what appears to be Shepherd's own vivid imagination, his status as a learned man—as well as his firsthand experience with a Melungeon girl—lend a public credence to his theories on Melungeons; thus, his writing gained a clout similar to Dromgoole's as one of the earliest authentic studies of Melungeons.

The Melungeon Exposé: *Saturday Evening Post*

Few journalists following these early writers discuss doing their own field research for their articles on Melungeons. Writers simply did not bother with fieldwork, or if they did, they found nothing about which they might write. As a result, the early writings on Melungeons became sanctified as the authoritative ones. This is particularly true in the case of Dromgoole, and only moderately less so with Shepherd. In the same way that Dromgoole borrowed liberally in her own historical renderings of Melungeons, antecedents to Dromgoole respun—or many times, simply repeated—her words. In this way, the popular literature on Melungeons became a cycle of conjecture published as fact. The wave of writings that followed these early writings offer little original information; at the same time, the very fact of their publication gives the illusion of a growing, cumulative knowledge.

The most significant of these journalistic offshoots is the infamous 1947 feature article on Melungeons in the *Saturday Evening Post*. Written by William Worden, the article received unprecedented national exposure and continues to be viewed by residents of Hancock County as a blight on their community. Most egregious to individuals in Sneedville—then and now—is the fact that this widely circulated national portrayal of Melungeons depicts the community as uneducated, primitive, and poor—with more than a hint that they may also be mixed race.

Worden's article is written with the same kind of self-proclaimed clout found in Dromgoole's work, due mostly to the photographic layout included in his piece. However, questions exist regarding whether or not Worden even visited Hancock County. According to Winkler (2004), local historian William Grohse claims that Worden did not visit the area but, instead, relied on notes by his photographer. Ivey (1976) also comments on Worden's sloppy research, suggesting that any interviewing he might have done was slim at best. Still Worden assures readers at the outset of his article: "About the people of Newman's Ridge and Blackwater Swamp just one fact is indisputable: There are such strange people"(Worden 1947). Worden then proceeds to show absolutely no evidence of such, either through observations or interactions with people. Instead most of his article is bloated with a recap of origin theories, stories from Dromgoole's extended study of Melungeons (though he questions their legitimacy at the same time that he rehashes them), and Shepherd's legal suit. When he does describe an unflattering scene of downtown Sneedville, it is difficult to distinguish observation from concoction:

In Sneedville on a "public day" when a lawing of some interest is under way in the county courthouse, many country people come to town from the rich farms along the Clinch River bottoms. Walking among them along the one muddy main street or leaning against the stone wall around the courthouse square will be other dark people—old women withered or excessively fat, inclined to talk very fast in musical voices; old men spare and taciturn, thin-lipped, rather like Indians, but not quite like them. Either they have some Latin characteristics or the effect of the legend is to make the stranger think they have. Some few of them—the daughters of these people are very often lovely, soft and feminine, in striking contrast to the bony appearance of most mountain women—live in the town. Of them, their neighbors say, "Well, they don't talk about it, but I happen to know her pappy used to make whiskey up on the ridge"; or, "He might not tell you, but he never came to town from Vardy until he was growed" (Worden 1947).

The photographic spread in the article captures nothing uniquely Melungeon; instead the images feature members of the Hancock County community, none of whom openly identified as Melungeon. Of course like those before him, Worden dealt with the daunting issue of writing about a topic that was not openly acknowledged. He even closes his article with a vague story that decorates his ambiguity related to Melungeons with creative license:

> In the small Tennessee hill towns, now and then, a dark man will talk to a stranger, tell a few incidents heard or seen on Newman's Ridge or advise him, "See ___. If anybody knows, he will." Only ___ never does. A lovely woman may even, looking straight at the visitor with gray eyes, say, "My own grandfather had some Indian blood and perhaps some Spanish. We don't know much about the family but there is a story that some of De Soto's men—". The lady may have small hands and feet, high cheekbones, straight hair and olive skin, and a regal carriage. She may talk for some time and tell much that is written in no books, some fact, some hearsay, some the most fanciful legend. But one word she will never say. She will never say, "Malungeon" (Worden 1947).

Worden's article on Melungeons relies almost entirely on secondary sources. His writing is typical of many of the articles to follow in that writers make statements or take arbitrary photographs to authenticate their work, but they offer little substantiation that they actually encounter Melungeons. These early works are emblematic of the manufacture of reality that exists in the literature on Melungeons; if an anecdote citing an early source is repeated enough, it promises a kind of truth that never existed in the first place. When it involves finding Melungeons in Hancock County, journalists appear to come, see little, and resort to secondary sources — peppering their stories with remnants from healthy imaginations and the most minute observations.

Thus the Melungeons constructed by the media are illusory, an amalgamation of anecdote, imagination, and creative license. Sovine (1982) characterizes this as a process whereby "most writers heard the legend, read the sources derived from secondary sources, and published yet another mythical account of the mysterious Melungeons in east Tennessee." What occurs in this mythical reproduction of the Melungeon story is the development of themes that contribute to the grand narrative of Melungeons. This narrative embodies a range of tropes that provide a cumulative caricature of Melungeons.

CHAPTER TWO

Melungeons and Media Representation

While most unsolved mysteries hold a limited interest in the popular imagination, the Melungeon story forges on, releasing a slew of synonyms that evoke their alleged enigmatic nature. Writers depict Melungeons as unusual, rare, mystical, strange, exotic, colorful, puzzling, hidden, forgotten, unknown, vanishing, secretive, fascinating, peculiar, odd, sinister, dark, tribal, and clannish. Writers revel in redundancy when describing Melungeons. Despite hundreds of different popular articles on Melungeons over the last one-hundred-plus years, the depictions are remarkably consistent. In the 1890s headlines promise stories of "A Strange Tennessee People." In the 1940s writers continue to talk about the "Mystery Men of the Mountains," and a 2002 headline reads: "The Melungeon Mystery Remains Unsolved."

Scholarship on the representation of Melungeons in popular media is limited. Winkler (2004) and Ivey (1976) provide the greatest breadth in their analysis of written sources, although both tend to focus more on historically significant writings rather than on the cultural meanings embedded in the written representations in general. Winkler's work is more current; thus he deals with important shifts in representations that weren't available when Ivey wrote her dissertation. Still, Winkler's work shies away from any kind of critical analysis of the social construction of identity vis-à-vis the popular media. Sovine's (1982) work provides a far more critical analysis of the manipulation of sources, although her presentation of content is rather telegraphic and includes only a brief analysis in the opening discussion. The analysis she provides, however, continues to be relevant and can be applied to articles that have been published in the last two decades. Vande Brake (2001) provides an overview of Melungeon characters in fiction that tends to be more descriptive than analytical.

In this chapter, I employ text from media representations from 1880 to the present to examine ways in which the media reproduce the Melungeon legend through an inspired repetition of fanciful tropes. My analysis of media portrayals of Melungeons delineates specific themes that present an image of Melungeons as fugitives from normative society whose history is unknown and whose presence is disappearing. Early Melungeons are rendered as primordial savages who find sanctuary in the swamps and ridges of the Appalachian Mountains. This picture changes little from 1880 to the late 1960s, when an outdoor drama on Melungeons is staged in Hancock County, Tennessee. Though the media continue to perpetuate the traditional mythical image of the Melungeon, new themes emerge in the 1960s to create a Melungeon whose primitive isolation resulted from racial discrimination. In the 1960s drama, Melungeons are heroic, and, in the media, Melungeons become a lure to draw tourists to Hancock County. By the 1990s Melungeon representations are further compounded by new twists on old themes. In particular, Melungeons become ever more exotic in portrayals of swarthy Appalachians who hail from Mediterranean seamen. As thousands of individuals begin to invest personally in the Melungeon story, they come to occupy an important space in media representations. However the new Melungeons do little to alter the fundamentals of the Melungeon legend; instead, many of the legendary themes simply serve as fodder for individuals to shape their own individual and collective histories. A critical analysis of hundreds of Melungeon articles yields an incredible truth — the Melungeon story is a respindled yarn with little or no basis in ethnographic reality. As I examine the context in which the earliest Melungeon articles were written, I argue that the media manufactured a Melungeon legend that has little to do with any lived experiences of an identifiable group of people.

The Pilgrimage

One of the most common tropes in journalistic writing about Melungeons is the pilgrimage, whereby writers strive to validate that Melungeons *do* exist. The most convincing validation, of course, is for writers to actually see and interact with Melungeons, yet few writers offer convincing firsthand accounts. The fallback to actually finding Melungeons tends to be using descriptive accounts of trying to find Melungeons; thus one's pilgrimage becomes what folklorist Brunvand (1991) calls a "validating formula" — a tactic to persuade audiences of legendary truths. In addition to posing as a kind of corroboration, the pilgrimage to Hancock County adds an element of suspense that works particularly well with the Melungeon legend.

In most of these articles, journalists typically do not have a lot to report once arriving, but their introductions adopt a pioneer motif, suggesting an exciting and sometimes precarious voyage. One article begins, "We parked and hoofed it more than a mile into the woods, stepping up the pace after noticing the tracks of a big cat, perhaps a mountain lion, in the dried mud" (Watson 1997). Another journalist introduces her mission to "search for the Melungeons" as one in which a "cityfied writer goes looking in the mountains for the truth about one of the Blue Ridge's unsolved mysteries" (Schroeder 1991). As with most writers who visit Hancock County in the 1990s, Schroeder reports a formulaic trek that involves visits to the Vardy school and church, the Mahala Mullins relocated log cabin, graveyards, Newman's Ridge, and brief interactions with the handful of individuals from Hancock County who, beginning in the 1990s, proudly claim their Melungeon descent. The conclusion is predictable: there is nothing new to tell, and the mystery continues. Schroeder's article is interesting in that her writing on Melungeons is well-researched, evenhanded, and intellectually astute. She is not naïve or particularly sensationalistic, yet she is a typical example of the ways in which journalists recycle the Melungeon story to contribute to a media-generated legend with enduring popular appeal.

One article (Melungeons 1981) reports a visit by former US Representative, Joe L. Evins, to "Melungeonland." The early ring of a Willy Wonka adventure morphs into a more reflective tone as Evins's journey progresses: "Evins didn't say so, but it was obvious when he struck out alone on the dusty road toward Sneedville that he wanted to soak up an atmosphere that had caught him in its legendary spell" (Melungeons 1981). The article refers to a tour of sites presumably inhabited by modern Melungeons, with several stops that yield rather mundane encounters with the beautiful people (Melungeons 1981). In each instance the author crafts descriptions that appear to be based largely on a blend of observation and historical imagination. The first stop was an abandoned house with dilapidated chimney, a site that leads the writer to the conclusion: "The man of the house, whose wife by custom always walked three steps behind him, was either too tired or too old to rebuild it". Near the deserted house, a 110-year-old Melungeon — "the oldest of them all" — warmed himself by a fire, as the writer testifies: "Typical of the early Melungeons, he made good whiskey at his still. And he was a practical man. When his wife died, he married the next-door widow. She was true to the cause and when he fired up his still, she would hang the family wash out front to hide the operation from the curious passersby on the road" (Melungeons 1981).

The next Melungeon family visited by Evins regaled him with stories about walking twenty-five miles a day while preparing squirrel stew. Finally the expedition ends with a visit to the house of a Melungeon widow. Though one wonders if there was any conversation at all, the author sums up the tour with a labored contemplation of a photograph on the wall that "told much about the mysterious Melungeons: Every other child was olive skinned or white."

Though few writers can compete with Dromgoole's early hyperbolic prose, a handful inflate the pioneer trope into a more dramatic pilgrimage tale. Louise Davis, a journalist whose articles resulted from at least a day or two in Hancock County, embeds her writing with reflections on Melungeon sensitivities regarding media representations. Yet her own entrée into Hancock County borders on the theatrical:

> A photographer and I set out to talk to these shy people and, if possible, to break down their longstanding refusal to have their picture made. In part, we succeeded. We found that the dark people are indeed there, pocketed mysteriously in the mountains where tow headed Anglo-Saxon children fill most of the schools. But the sullen eyes of Anglo-Saxon citizens (who make up 99 percent of the population of Hancock County) followed every move we made, and even the sheriff challenged the photographer's right to make a picture of the courthouse. The tragedy of the "lost race" was thick around us. "Every eye in the valley is watching you," one of our kind guides (who asked not to be identified) said after we had left Sneedville, the county seat, and risen over Newman's Ridge

to dip down the back side where the few identifiable members of the race live (Davis 1963).

Peter Dunn, whose article appeared in the *London Sunday Times Magazine*, immediately launches into an altercation as introduction to his surly portrait of Hancock County: "A man shouted angrily in a valley called Snake Hollow. . . . Archie 'Mutt' Bell, tall, thin and with dark skin, ran down the dirt road from his tobacco farm, shaking a tobacco stick. 'You will not take photographs,' Bell shouted. 'Just you give me that film.' John Bulmer, wary of the man's rage, handed over an unexposed film. Bell waited around, pacing, then ran up the road to get his car. 'I'm going for the police,' he said. We drove off, fast, in the opposite direction scattering chickens and the bright red cardinal birds" (Dunn 1967).

Dark, Beautiful People

Having presumably found Melungeons, authors are under pressure to describe them in a way that perpetuates their exotic appeal. These descriptions tend to be widely variable. In the words of the author of the *Littell's* article, Melungeons are a "tall, straight, well-formed people of a dark copper color, with Circassian features, but wooly heads and other similar appendages of our negro" (Melungens 1849). By 1912 another writer drafts a very different look for Melungeons:

> They are of a swarthy complexion, with prominent cheekbones, jet-black hair, generally straight but at times having a slight tendency to curl, and the men have heavy black beards. They have deep-set, dark brown eyes. Their frames are well built and some of the men are fine specimens of physical manhood. They are seldom fat. Their lips are not noticeably thicker nor their feet broader than those of pure Caucasians, and although their hair is sometimes wavy it is seldom, if ever, kinky. Some

of the small boys with their uncombed hair, dirty faces and wide, staring eyes look like young Indians fresh from their smoky wigwams. The girls, however, with their brown eyes, rosy cheeks and heavy black locks are good examples of natural beauty. (Converse 1912)

The prismatic appearance of Melungeons serves as a common theme that may well reflect a writer's interpretation of a multiethnic group of people. Indeed, if Melungeons existed as a tri-racial isolate that intermarried, the notion of a distinct-looking group of people is unlikely. Regardless of the specific characterizations, the more significant point rests with the palpable agenda shared by all of these articles to establish what becomes an unquestioned truth in the media — that Melungeons are dark and different. This notion of ethnic ambiguity provides one of the earliest and most important foundations of the Melungeon legend. Though there is little uniformity in the specifics of Melungeons' physical appearance overall, writers consistently wax poetic on the physical attractiveness of Melungeon women. When it comes to describing Melungeon women, writers repeatedly reflect on the women's preternatural primal beauty. Shepherd's work on the Melungeon case sets the stage for this sexualization of Melungeon women. He writes about his defendant:

She was a dark brunette. She had a suite of black hair, which was coveted by all the girls who knew her. Her form was petite, and yet, withal was so plump and so well developed as to make her an irresistibly charming young woman. She was most beautiful of face, and had a rich black eye, in whose depths the sunbeams seemed to gather. When she loosed her locks they fell, almost reaching the ground, and shone in the sunlight, or quivered like the glamour which the full moon throws on the placid water. She was the essence of grace and loveliness. Our hero fell in love with this delightful young woman. . . .

She knew nothing about the ways of the world. She was totally ignorant of the prevailing fashions of dress; she did not
know what a corset was or how it was worn, whether over or
under the dress. She had spent most of her life in the forest
alone. . . . She knew nothing whatever of the arts of fashion-
able women, in making for themselves attractive forms and
figures by skillful lacing—she was simply an uncouth, an un-
sophisticated, unmade up, natural girl from the backwoods,
a girl withal, possessed of a strikingly beautiful face, and a
figure that by proper development and dress was capable of
being molded into a form that would please the most fastidious. She was very much like her mother, and possessed all
the charms and graces she did, but they were undeveloped.
(Shepherd 1913)

Writers following Shepherd reproduce these overwrought
accounts of beautiful Melungeon women with few excep-
tions. In one article Sneedville historian Grohse comments,
"Pioneers fancied [that] in the Melungeon women they
were again viewing the profiles of ancient Egyptian queens"
(Grohse 1969). Another stricken author proclaims that "Melungeon women and their daughters have an olive beauty,
enhanced by hazel eyes and black hair that seemingly is
unmatched anywhere else" (Yarbrough 1979). A third description focuses on the "soft, round-faced beauty" of Melungeon women that stands in "striking contrast to the
lean-faced, bony look of many mountain women of Anglo-
Saxon descent" (Davis 1970).

The Primitive

Even when it's not entirely clear whether or not a writer visited Hancock County or talked to people who lived there,
popular articles about Melungeons are replete with geographical descriptions that are suggestive of being there. Articles refer to "back coves," "isolated ridges," "snake dens,"

"dark hills," and "savage wilderness." These descriptions hint at a visual authority that writers fall back on to elevate the suspense factor when real Melungeons are nowhere to be found. In addition to being used as strategy in travel tales, these topographical narrations almost exclusively posit an isolated and untamed landscape. In this way writers create an image of primitive isolation in their descriptions, painting Melungeons as wild and uncultivated.

Journalists characterize Melungeons as a colony, tribe, race, clan, breed, and, in at least one case, a species: "You must know that within some 10 miles of this owl's nest, there is a watering-place, known hereabouts as Blackwater Spring. It is situated in a narrow gorge, scarcely half a mile wide, between Powell's Mountain and the Copper Ridge and is, as you may suppose, almost inaccessible. Now this gorge and the tops and sides of the adjoining mountains are inhabited by a singular species of the human animal called Melungens" (Melungens 1849).

Though the agenda of the *Littell's* article has already been discussed as dubious, the author is not alone in employing an unforgiving terrain to underscore themes of uncultivated seclusion. One writer claims that Melungeons "took to the hills, the isolated peaks of the uninhabited mountains, the corners of the earth, as it were, where, huddled together, they became a law unto themselves, a race indeed separate and distinct from the several races inhabiting the state of TN" (Melungeons 1890).

In many of these geographical portraits, the southern Appalachian landscape exists in tandem with the Melungeons who inhabit it. Ball, for example, claims that Melungeon dwellings were "crude, sometimes [the] insides of cliffs." She asserts that Melungeons "often prefer wild, unfrequented hill country" (Ball 1973). Another writer states that the names of Hancock County communities — Snake Hollow and Blackwater Swamp the most commonly invoked — are "synonymous with the mysterious olive-skinned dwellers" (Yarbrough 1980). The mountains, hollows, and swamps serve as shields for Melungeon isolation and duplicity. One writer points out, with regard to the Melungeons' "savage wilderness," that "the mountains have sheltered them and kept their secret" (Tigue 1969). Another claims that "now and then, strangers failed to come back from the ridge or the swamp" (Worden 1947). In a similar vein the aforementioned journalist, Dunn, continues his hostile portrayal of Hancock County when he describes its geography: "To sophisticated northerners the area of Hancock County which encloses Snake Hollow is a joke place . . . its rough slopes concealing the moon-shining lives of unkempt hillbillies, indiscriminate shotgun blasts echoing in the wooded mountains" (Dunn 1967).

The mountains act as realms of concealment, with much of the lore relating to Melungeons' escape from white settlers. One article states that "they retreated into their mountain caves as the white men came to the mountains of east Tennessee imposing near-slave restrictions on them" (Brandeis Professor). Another makes a more direct connection between these natural refuges and the savage nature of Melungeons as they were driven away by the white man: "As the white pioneers made the Melungeons life more difficult by confiscating their developed land, they retreated to the most remote coves clinging together and protecting themselves as best they could. The reviled outsiders and marriages tended to be confined among Melungeon families. Because of the enforced isolation their way of life remained primitive and austere until the last 20 or 30 years" (Herbermann 1994). In addition to hiding Melungeons, the mountains represent lairs for sordid activities: "There are stories of Melungeons who lived in mountainside caves when the first white settlers arrived and numerous stories of violent deeds there" (Davis 1963).

Melungeons and Media Representation

Much of the popular literature sustains the notion of a feral Melungeon subsistence. In one article a special correspondent provides a particularly egregious example of Melungeons as animalistic: "They are grossly ignorant, beastly in their habits and weak physically and mentally. . . . To allay their terrible sufferings they resort to mud baths, often spending days in the wallow like hogs" (Melungeons 1890). Few writers neglect to mention Snake Hollow in their narratives about Melungeons in Hancock County: "Trapped in poverty, snubbed by their fair-skinned neighbors, some of them withdrew to the poor land along Snake Hollow, deep in the rattlesnake-infested gorge in the shadow of towering Newman's Ridge" (Davis 1963).

Outlaws

At the same time that some writers employ geography to denote a sense of the untamed Melungeon, legions of them focus more explicitly on Melungeon lawlessness and aggression. The nature of the depictions varies, ranging from descriptions of Melungeon feuding and moonshining to dire warnings to avoid Melungeon territory altogether. Writing repeatedly portrays Melungeons as barbaric, weapon-carrying outlaws. Many of these accounts relate to folk stories about Melungeons breaking the law through moonshining: "They always carried guns or knives and many a bloody murder and foul crime has been committed in this region. By its lawlessness and bloodshed this section came to be known to the inhabitants of the more peaceful valleys to the east of the Clinch as 'yan side' . . . . Up to 2 decades ago, whiskey flowed like water in the Blackwater country and moonshining was a common occupation. A stranger who ventured into that region in those days did so at the risk of his life." (Converse 1912).

Another writer addresses the presumed problem of theft by Melungeons. Within a few sentences, he manages to disparage Melungeons, draw from the geographical tropes discussed earlier, and warn outsiders to avoid Melungeons at all costs: "No one, not even the sheriff of Hancock County, dared to enter their domain. Treated with a mixture of derision and respect, the "nigger stealers" were left alone in "a country that seemed so much like Hell. . . . Melungeon—it's a name for a separate generation of mankind in these mountains" (Stinson 1973).

In a number of characterizations of Melungeon waywardness, their presumed violent tendencies are naturalized as part of their inborn nature. In a 1937 article that laments the changed Melungeon, Aswell remembers when it was unsafe for white men to venture into Melungeon territory: "As late as 1820 it was not safe for a white man to cross Melungeon territory. He had about 1 chance in 10 of coming through with a whole skin. All that is changed now. Inbreeding and bad blood have smothered the Melungeon fire" (Aswell 1937). Davis is more direct regarding the seemingly innate temperament of Melungeons, stating that their legendary crimes "grew more out of a child-like amorality than from any malice" (Davis 1963). In a particularly colorful description in which Melungeon violence becomes naturalized, Worden notes: "Now and then when strangers approached the ridge too closely or ventured into Blackwater Swamp, they used the long rifles which seemed almost like parts of their bodies, so naturally were they carried. . . . Now and then, strangers failed to come back from the ridge or the swamp" (Worden 1947).

As is evident in the commentary above, cautionary tales to avoid Melungeon territory are embedded in most discussions of Melungeon hostility. For example Dromgoole offers a vivid warning: "Mountain legend says that if a man is fool enough to wander into Melungeon country and if he comes back without being shot, he is sure to wizen and perish with some ailment nobody could name" (Dromgoole

1891). In a later, and equally questionable, observation, another journalist describes his journey to Hancock County: "It is said that for many years to enter in to Melungeon country was quick death. Evidence of this guntotin' can be seen today as revealed by the multitude of bullet riddled road signs marking the road ways around Sneedville" (Harvey 1951).

The Mystery

An extension of the notion of the renegade Melungeon is the cult of mystery and secrecy that surrounds the group. Embedded in tales of Melungeon menace are implications that a deeply ingrained mystery prohibits Melungeons from revealing their identity to or interacting with outsiders. This is most evident in journalistic accounts constantly colored by allegations that the very term "Melungeon" invoked peril. Melungeon is most often referred to as a fighting word in the popular media, and advisories to readers abound. What is most curious about the assertion that use of the term Melungeon was an unspeakable offense is the fact that in most cases journalists were not using the term openly with those who might have been Melungeons, or, at least, were not reporting repercussions for using the word.

In some accounts, writers acknowledge outright that the individuals they seek do not call themselves Melungeons nor identify as Melungeons. Still the admission is typically unapologetic. In many cases, journalists simply state that the Melungeons do not know their own history. One writer states about Melungeon heritage that "the Melungeons won't tell. They can't—for they don't know" (Smith and Rogers 1966). Another refers to the Melungeons' "bewildered lack of knowledge about themselves" (Dunn 1967). And another recounts: "Not one of them was able to tell me any of their history, at least, not one did" (Vincent 1964).

Journalists also commonly pose, as an alternate possibility

to Melungeon ignorance of their past, the explanation that Melungeons just don't want to *talk* about their history. These explanations provide an equally viable out for journalists who are unable to unearth problematic histories. One writer states, "Very few of Melungeon descent care to admit to it, and several people declined to discuss their ancestry when asked to do so" (Canfield 1987). Davis provides the most thorough example of this proclivity for journalistic distraction in her interaction with a Melungeon woman:

> There are few "pure Melungeons" left today. The Melungeons still there deeply resent outsiders who pry into their ancestry and pontificate on their intelligence and industry. They themselves refuse to discuss the matter, and few will talk to reporters on any subject. The Melungeons themselves a clannish lot who are said to talk freely among themselves of their mysterious beginnings, are silent when outsiders broach the subject. A slight, engaging woman, hospitable and kind, she became inscrutable as Buddha when we asked her about Portuguese or Spanish settlers in the area, and, finally about Melungeons. "I don't know anything about that," she said, suddenly wide-eyed and innocent. "I don't know about such as that" (Davis 1963).

In at least a few accounts, writers encounter the complete denial that Melungeons even exist. A local motel owner, for example, states that the Melungeon phenomenon is "hogwash" and, simply, an invention of Will Allen Dromgoole: "The word 'Melungeon' is Miss Dromgoole's headwork and everyone's copied it since" (Dunn 1967). Another account reports that the issue of identity simply does not matter to the residents of Hancock County: "They are what they are" (Smith and Rogers 1966). Hancock County respondents repeatedly tell journalists that they did not hear the term "Melungeon"—in relation to themselves or their neighbors—until they were adults. One woman claims,

Melungeons and Media Representation

"The people who are foreign to this area know more about it than we do ourselves" (Endicott 1970). The same woman, in another interview, claims that the "hill people" who heard about Melungeons simply knew them in the ways that other Appalachians did—as part of a legend used to frighten children: "Better be good or the Melungeons will get you!" (Yarbrough 1972). Another local man explains: "These theories have all been brought on by outside people. . . . Until a few years ago, this wasn't even talked about. . . . It doesn't seem like many people in this area are interested in their ancestry" (Endicott 1970).

In one article a journalist encounters two individuals who decry the Melungeon phenomenon. One states, "I've lived here all my life and I don't know what a Melungeon is," while the second offers a more cynical response: "I may have dark skin and dark eyes and black hair, but so do a lot of people. Hell, it's all just theory" (Melungeons 1987). And, in typical journalistic form, one author couches a farmer's lack of interest in heritage in a rather disingenuous portrayal that conveys a well-established, imagined Melungeon lifestyle: "Monroe Collins, a tenant farmer at the foot of Bunches Trace . . . doesn't give a hoot about his people's origin. He'd rather pour water into groundhog holes along the creek, flushing his quarry, and convert the animal either into stew for dinner or a pet on a leash in his yard" (Yarbrough 1972).

So while journalists write with the presumption that Melungeons exist, they also acknowledge the ready denial of that existence. Yet, rather than draw the conclusion that the mysterious Melungeons may be more a product of legend than of reality, journalists deduce that individuals are either ignorant of or unwilling to confess their identity. This becomes a significant strategy for the media to legitimate their work, while it also affirms the idea of a cult of secrecy understood today to be integral to Melungeon identity.

The Disappearing Melungeon

A similar rationale for writing about the mysteriously absent Melungeon might explain the equally abundant tales of the disappearing Melungeon. Few articles refrain from reflections on culture change when discussing Melungeons, be it related to migration, intermarriage, or cultural assimilation. Take, for example, a sampling of headlines of Melungeon articles over time:

A Strange Tennessee People: The Malungeons and Their Customs — Changes Wrought by Time

Vardy Valley's Melungeons Last of a Dying Breed

A Vanishing Race

The Mystery of the Melungeons: Why Are They Vanishing?

Mysterious E-T Mountain Clan Becoming Extinct

The Melungeons: A Race Headed for Extinction

The Secret of the Melungeons Buried Deeper Now as Progress Takes Toll of Mystery People

Most of the Melungeons are Either Gone . . . or Going

Mysterious Hill Folk Vanishing

The Mystery of the Melungeons: The Story of a Vanishing People of East Tennessee

Mystery People of Hancock County: Melungeons' Ways Are Passing

The Melungeons Have Left Newman's Ridge, but Their Heritage Remains

In some cases authors present change as a civilizing force that Melungeons both want and need. Dromgoole, for example, frequently invokes the railroad as the agent of change that Melungeons yearn for in a "half-regretful, half-pathetic way": "They all look for it (the train), constantly and always, as if they expect to see, some glad day, the brunt of the iron track, the glorious herald of prosperity and knowledge, come creeping up the mountain, horseback or afoot, bringing joy to the cabin even of the outcast and ostracized Melungeon" (Dromgoole 1890a). In general, references to culture change also reflect a nostalgia for Melungeons' simple way of life in the face of the inevitable encroachment of civilization. Davis bemoans the impact of the outside world: "Electricity threads the mountains and valleys now, and television antennae sprout out of the lonely cabin roofs like giant briars to trap the outside world" (Davis 1963).

It is significant that the preoccupation with culture change begins as early as the first writings on Melungeons and continues today. Over time writers agonize over finding "pure" or "real" Melungeons. The mechanism of change offers a ready rationalization for what most journalists probably believe — that Melungeons do not exist as a distinct-looking, geographically bounded group. Davis, for example, claims that Melungeons have become "a race so rare that Hancock County citizens can point out only two or three families with certainty. And they prefer not to do that" (Davis 1963). Others concur, stating that "inter-marriage with others has made a 'pure' Melungeon hard to find" (Mysterious Melungeons 1970) and that "finding a Melungeon with the traditional physical characteristics is nearly impossible" (Canfield 1987). In a curious spin on the change theme, another journalist reflects: "Deep in the hills of northeast Tennessee once lied [sic] a mysterious, dark people called Melungeons. They exist no more, yet they will never die as long as there are reporters to write about them and tourists to seek them out" (Melungeons 1987).

Interestingly, this writer's contemplation is one of the few to concede that the presence of Melungeons depends more on public imagination than on reality. Indeed, the premise of the Melungeon as the noble savage becomes well-established by the early 1900s. The many other related elements of the Melungeon narrative become rote over the next century, resulting in a media phantasm of the mysterious Melungeon. This pre-modern narrative holds layered meanings for individuals who begin to people the legend in the 1970s when the Melungeon story is staged in Hancock County.

CHAPTER THREE

Playing the First Melungeons

Melungeon legend transformed in a fundamental way in the mid-twentieth century. The change involved the staging of the outdoor drama about Melungeons, *Walk Toward the Sunset*, in Hancock County in the mid-1960s. With the drama, Melungeonness secured a public presence in the community for the first time, and the media gained a foothold to talk about Melungeons in a tangible way. The inception of the play launched a process by which individuals tentatively laid claim to a Melungeon identity and the community as a whole began to stake claims in the Melungeon debate. This chapter explores the transition of the Melungeon legend with the establishment of the outdoor drama. I focus on the process by which the drama and the topic of Melungeons were formally introduced to the Hancock County public and reproduced through the local, regional, and national media. I then draw from interviews conducted in Hancock County to reflect on local responses to the drama and the phenomenon of Melungeonness.

Walk Toward the Sunset

In 1966 a small group of individuals working on the Hancock County Resource Development Committee collaborated with Carson Newman College professors Gary Farley and Joe Mack High to identify potential resources available to aid economic development in Hancock County. The study resulted in the proposal of an outdoor drama based on the Melungeon story. According to Ivey (1976), which cites Farley and High's 1966 report extensively, they concluded that, given the terrain and isolation of Hancock County, industrial development was unlikely and "attention should be given to other types of possible economic input." They focused on one possible type:

> A natural possibility for such input is the idea of a drama featuring the mystery of the Melungeon settlement in the county. Interest in these people has been recently heightened by Jesse Stuart's novel, *Daughter of a Legend*. Similar projects have been successful nearby—Big Stone Gap, Berea, and Abingdon. This proximity to other successful dramas should enhance the chances of success in Hancock. In addition, the natural spin-off from the drama would be an outlet for handicraft items. It would also provide the basis for the development of food and lodging services for tourists and other economic impetus. (quoted in Ivey 1976)

Claude Collins, a prominent leader on the development committee, recalls the meeting in which a local pastor suggested the topic of Melungeons for the drama: "And my pastor spoke up and said, you have a good story. Just tell it. And somebody asked him what it was. And he said, tell the story of the Melungeons. And I thought, oh dear. They'll run him outta here next week" (Interview by author). According to Ivey (1976), the sensitivity of organizing a drama about Melungeons was not lost on High and Farley, as they wrote: "This project is not without potential problems. There is a history of tension between the Melungeons and the Scotch-Irish settlers. . . . Parenthetically, some of the town's people reacted negatively to this book" (quoted in Ivey 1976). Farley and High continued to recommend that the local leaders of what came to be organized as the

Hancock County Drama Association (HCDA) seek Melungeon support in the endeavor.

As longtime residents of Hancock County, Collins and other HCDA leaders realized that a drama about Melungeons would need to be introduced carefully to the community. According to one HCDA member, the strategy was to familiarize the community with the drama through weekly articles in the *Hancock County Post* and in public forums and meetings:

> We went around and visited schools, sort of a small group of us, explaining what the play was about and so on ahead of time. We worked, I guess, a year, close to a year, just getting the people acquainted and talking about it. And I know there was one man over here, he got so mad he couldn't stand it. He was in one of the meetings, and he got mad and he left, you know. Another thing, too, that made it pretty good was that Martha Collins was a Melungeon. Everyone knew she was a Melungeon, and she was the President of Sneedville Bank. She was the treasurer at that time. And, you know, with her backing too, and her so active, because she wanted to see the name Melungeon more respected. (Interview by author)

Indeed records from the *Post* indicate that articles about the drama were regularly included in the paper, beginning in December 1967. Corinne and Dora Bowlin wrote a regular column with updates on the drama, as did Mayor Charles Turner. The early articles about the drama tend to be brief and informational, and, interestingly, they do not mention the proposed topic of Melungeons for the play. Attention, instead, is paid to public meetings about the drama and invitations for the community to attend. In addition early articles mention the importance of community support and cooperation and focus on how the drama will benefit the community. It is not until February 8, 1968, that the *Post* formally announces that the drama will focus on

Melungeons. The announcement is delivered in the form of a rather elaborate treatise by Reverend R. B. Conner on the advantages of producing a play on Melungeons. The article begins with the question "Why have a drama about the Melungeons in Hancock County?" and then lists six reasons:

1. This is the county's greatest asset at the present time.

2. If we do not stage such a drama some near-by county will.

3. The local drama committee can and will see that nothing goes into the drama to hurt any of our citizens.

4. Newman's Ridge, formerly called "New Man's Ridge," because of the discovery of these new people living there, has been recognized as the main seat of the Melungeon colony.

5. Such a drama will benefit every citizen of Hancock County and neighboring counties.

6. The struggle of the Melungeon people is in many ways closely similar to the struggle of all people. (Why Have a Drama 1968)

Conner goes on to ask "Who should be interested in a drama in Hancock County?," providing six more answers:

1. The Melungeons, those with some Indian heritage, the negroes and the so-called pure Anglo-Saxon.

2. The poorest citizens as they will profit most.

3. The land owners, for the end result will be better roads.

4. The uneducated because the inflow of tourists will broaden their vision.

5. The educated who are interested in seeing the reputation of our county raised to a higher level.

Playing the First Melungeons

6. All business men, merchants, service station oper-
ations, motel owners and those interested in oper-
ating eating establishments. (Why Have a Drama
1968)

Finally Conner ends with the question, "How will profits
come from the drama?" His prolonged answer includes
providing employment, showcasing crafts, and promoting
tourism. His final answer focuses on the more abstract
notion of community pride, phrased as a request that the
drama not create divisiveness. Conner states, "I would like
to see this undertaking lifted above all party politics and
group prejudices. This is not a project for and by a few; it
must be an undertaking for and by all the people of Hancock County and adjoining counties, then it can be an effort that will unite us all as nothing else has" (Why Have
a Drama 1968). Conner's article is interesting in that, as
he was the first to formally introduce the topic of Melungeons, it anticipates and attempts to forestall potential acrimony over the topic.

After the Conner article, the *Post* did not publish anything further about the drama or Melungeons until the special July 4, 1968, edition, titled, "Hancock County—The
Land of Enchantment." This edition focuses almost exclusively on Hancock County's local history—including the
Melungeons—in pieces with titles such as "The County
that Time Forgot" and "The Land of Mystery." This edition
represents the first attempt by the paper to sell both Hancock County and the mystique of the Melungeons to the
local public. In a nostalgic narrative on Hancock County,
local historian Alton Greene offers readers a virtual tour
through the mountains. When he gets to Newman's Ridge,
he notes that "the air of mystery hangs like a morning
fog" and then assures readers that "even though you may
not be familiar with the history of this particular section,

I think you will sense an unusualness or catch the air of mystery that penetrates there. You are now in Melungeon country" (Greene 1968). Another local historian, William Grohse (1969), writes a later piece for the *Post* that primarily details local historical events, with some information on Melungeons. The special edition concludes with a reprint of an article from the *Tennessee Conservationist* titled "Melungeons."

The HCDA remained true to their promise to keep the local community informed about the drama, printing weekly updates in the *Post* beginning by March 1969. The articles tend to be straightforward, overviewing details of the most recent happenings and adding repeated entreaties to the public to donate time and/or money and to welcome outsiders who visit Hancock County during the play. Although the articles do not address any negativity expressed by the community toward the drama association, there is an underlying tone that serves as an ongoing reminder to the local community to show support for the drama. In addition to pleas for monetary support and good will, the *Post* launches a campaign to its readers to pay particular attention to the care of their homes and surroundings in preparation for the drama. In a column labeled, "Fair Warning," Hancock Countians are advised to take special heed of the annual "Clean Up-Fix Up-Paint Up" venture:

> The merchants and people of Sneedville especially, as well as everyone throughout the county should do an especially good job of cleaning up their property this year. The main reason for doing a good job is that "company is coming." Visitors will be in the county to see the Drama and to see some of our other main points of interest and beauty. So do your best and let's all get together this year to do a real fine job of cleaning up our county. Later this week and early next week pictures will be taken of some of the more unsightly places in

this area. Places that could use a good cleaning up or a paint job. Don't get caught in the picture . . . start your clean up now." (Fair Warning 1969)

In an editorial the following week, Grohse reiterates: "Everyone should take pride in their surroundings. They should keep their own surroundings clean. There is no excuse for throwing tin cans and garbage in front of a person's home. This reflects on our community and the inhabitants of the household. Tourists will be coming into our community. Some will have cameras. Some will take pictures of the trash-littered homes and display them for others to see. Would you want a picture of your home and surroundings published for all to see?" (Grohse 1969)

HCDA representatives also implore Hancock County citizens to be friendly to tourists. In the July 24, 1969, issue of the *Post*, Bowlin writes: "Let me urge all of you to be as courteous and friendly to the strangers who will be coming as you normally are to the people around you who you have known all your life. A smile will go a long way toward making visitors feel welcome." Well into the next year, drama leaders continue to prod the community. Mayor Turner, for example, reiterates this message to the community in a slightly stricter tone:

Anything that our community has accomplished has come as a result of following through and overcoming all obstacles and objections. Following through is not always easy. Sometimes it is most difficult. Very often it requires courage, inner strength and great will power. The success of the outdoor drama at this point can be attributed to the fact that there are a good number of people in our county who were willing to follow through. . . . I am proud of these people, I congratulate them, and I hope that the citizens of our town will be more seriously considering their effort and assisting in sustaining this progressive endeavor. To all who had seen to it that their property was looking its best on July 2, 3 and 4th and were out talking with visitors and driving them around, or helping in any way we are indeed grateful. These are those who would not choose to be a deterrent to progress but rather to in some manner sustain it. (Turner 1970)

One can only wonder to what extent these repeated appeals grew tiresome to the community. However well-intentioned, these media prompts had the specific purpose of trying to manufacture consent about the drama, when, in reality, the drama created fissures in the community. Still, for HCDA leaders the strategy seemed to work: the first seasons of the drama were well received by outsiders.

Melungeons and the Media Romance

The outdoor drama immediately captured the imagination of the press and the region. In numerous articles, writers reinvigorate the well-established tropes employed in journalistic accounts to that point. The legendary Melungeon clichés continue; however, new themes surface as well with the staging of *Walk Toward the Sunset*. Most notably the push for tourism heightens the discourse of romance and exoticism surrounding the Melungeons. In a series of articles encouraging tourists to see the play, Knoxville reporter Yarbrough promises intrigue and adventure. He announces the drama as the *News Sentinel*'s "most exotic adventure in its long Trip of the Month series" and follows with lavish description: "You've heard about and read about the mysterious Melungeons of Newman's Ridge whose origin is lost in romantic antiquity. Now you can see them and talk with them. Better still, you can see them perform in the new outdoor drama" (Yarbrough 1969a). Another reporter offers a similar tease: "If you haven't seen the Melungeon drama 'Walk Toward the Sunset' at Sneedville you should put it down as a must sometime this season. You have heard and wondered about the Melungeons all your life. So have your fathers and mothers, and your grandparents. Now you have a chance to see and talk with these people and be entertained by their dramatized story" (Vincent 1969). Most of the articles of the time suggest that the main draw to the outdoor drama is the opportunity to see actual Melungeons. In one feature on the drama, the writer states this about the audience: "What they want to see is not only the spectacle of Indian dances and Melungeon weddings on stage, under the stars. Most of all they want to get a good look at a real, live Melungeon" (Davis 1970). In a particularly maudlin appeal to tourists, a reporter named Tigue embellishes his writing with the invocation of real Melungeons. He begins with 108-year-old "living legend," Grandpap Mullins:

> Grandpap is one of the few citizens of the county who can recount old Melungeon legends. . . . Seeing a century of springs and summers pass has etched a beautiful dignity into the hollows and planes of his face. His wise, old reptilian eyes have seen many things, and now the eyes don't see at all—They have seen so much they are tired. . . . His hands, which have been mountain-strong, are now as delicate as porcelain. . . . And grandpap remembers what it was like to smell the first raw spring scent the breeze brings, the scent of brown earth being overturned by the plow. And maybe, far in the distance, he can hear the sounds of happy Melungeon children as they welcome the sun's return with uplifted faces." (Tigue 1969)

In his article, Tigue includes photographs of Mullins's face and hands, as well as a picture labeled "Melungeon Girl." He describes the girl as "typical of the beauty of the Melungeon women, whose appearance is characterized by olive skin, gray eyes, high cheek bones, and long dark hair." In the picture the girl is whittling, with unkempt hair and soiled clothes. Tigue ends his article with a predictable contemplation on the Melungeon mystery: "So the story of the Melungeons will be told. And sitting peaceably in the spring sun, Opal whittles. Perhaps she wonders in the long lost days of memory and heritage where her people were born. Or maybe, with a child's knowledge she knows" (Tigue 1969).

Reporters guarantee hospitality Melungeon style, including "mountain musicians playing the dulcimer and guitar and with ballads that will make you glad you came" (Yarbrough 1969b). In another article the list of activities expands to "Melungeon lectures at the courthouse, a display of medicinal herbs dug out of mountain soil by Melungeons and sold on the market, and Melungeon cemeteries bear the trademark of graveports — much like carports — over the remembered dead" (Yarbrough 1970). Other reporters promise native Melungeon handcrafts (Clark 1969), as well as the opportunity to "stop at the homes of local craftsmen to learn craftmaking skills first hand" (These People 1970). The most popular activity, however, was tours provided by a local resident, Claude Collins, to scout out Melungeons.

Writers dwell on the opportunity for escape vis-à-vis Melungeons and their drama. According to one reporter the escapism begins with the journey to the play: "A trip to Sneedville's 'WTTSS [Walk Toward the Sunset] brings back many of the simple sides of life. The drive to Sneedville is usually never congested except for an occasional roadside groundhog or maybe the glimpse of a small fox. The drive is slow and easy. The evening views are simple and natural for the most part. Even the trip works as a marvelous escape." Upon arriving, readers are promised continued elusion from modernity: "As you arrive at the ticket booth you are lured even deeper into the simple life by the vibrating notes of the dulcimer" (Head 1973). Davis comments that "there are no neon lights in town, no bars, and no junk stores" and quotes a visitor's reminiscence that "topping Clinch

Mountain and dropping down this valley is like seeing a Christmas card come alive" (Davis 1970). Another journalist elaborates on the natural setting of the play: "A mockingbird there also is no slouch. This bird and Molly Bowlin provide pre-performance music. Molly, who plays the dulcimer, stops before the play begins. But the mocker keeps on pouring it out right through dusk. . . . From where you sit looking down at the performance, the mocker is to the right rear, fairly close to where a horse was picking grass in a little cove. Far up above the cove is Newman's Ridge, the long-time home of the Melungeons. It's the finest natural backdrop you're likely to see" (Brewer 1970).

In addition to further romanticizing Melungeons, the media presentation of the drama introduces, or elaborates on, a pride and prejudice theme related to Melungeon identity. Though earlier articles periodically mention discrimination against Melungeons, the combined themes of historical oppression, overcoming adversity, and taking pride in being Melungeon emerge with a passion in media articles focusing on the drama. Indeed the drama itself centers on this premise. In the first act of the play, set in the aftermath of the American Revolution, white settlers banish a Melungeon couple from their land. The Melungeons join forces with the Cherokee, who offer them land on Newman's Ridge and assistance in their escape from white tyranny. The second act of the play forwards to the end of the Civil War and involves an ill-fated romance between a white war veteran and a Melungeon woman. The related story lines involve a legal battle over Melungeon timber rights and a smallpox outbreak that ravages the white community. With natural immunity to smallpox and armed with folk-healing wisdom, Melungeons revive the sick. As a result whites unify with Melungeons and restore their timber rights.[1]

In the media a slew of new adjectives emerge to detail

the experiences of Melungeon ancestors. Melungeons in history are said to be maligned, persecuted, ostracized, and disenfranchised. Journalists position the drama as a venue through which Melungeons are responding to an oppressive history. Writing about the content of the play, one reporter describes the Melungeon story as "one of a fight of courageous peoples to be left alone and freed from the ridicule of a dispassionate world" (Walk 1971). Another sums up the play as the "story of a brave, young woman in her fight to free her people from the ridicule and bigotry of outsiders who have tended to treat them with the same attitude often accorded minorities" (Ewing 1970).

In writing about the construction of the amphitheater, the media articles center on the idea of a determined, collective community spirit in Sneedville. Comparing volunteers to their pioneer forbearers, Juanita Glenn describes the community effort to create the site for the drama: "A hundred years or so ago, when some family on Newman's Ridge needed a home or a barn, his Melungeon neighbors would stage a 'working' and combining socializing with labor, soon would have the building completed. Something of the same sort went on last Friday at the site of a new amphitheater adjacent to Hancock County Elementary School, where the Melungeons' story will be told in an outdoor drama this summer" (Glenn 1969). Another writer declares that "this is where the local people put their shoulders to the wheel and said, 'We can do it'" (This and That 1969). The notion of a can-do cooperation that surmounts the odds becomes a metaphor for the Melungeons themselves: "With few natural resources beyond the beauty of their surroundings, their willingness to forget ancient animosities, and the will to work together, they presented *Walk Toward the Sunset*" (Clark 1969). Other journalists concur: "A town in danger of becoming impoverished and a mysterious race of people bordering on extinction have

Playing the First Melungeons

become uniquely bonded in a momentous effort that bridges over 100 years of mutual prejudice, fear and antagonism" (These People 1970).

The analogue to this dramatic demonstration of community determination is the notion that Melungeons are emerging with a proud self-identification. Yarbrough (1968) boasts that, with the drama, Melungeons "at long last may find an honored place in the American sun." He elaborates in a later article that Melungeons have "come out of hiding and now feel pride in their difference" (Yarbrough 1970). Another writer contends that the play will "lift the Melungeon name from shame to the hall of fame" (Price 1968). Story after story reports what seems to be an epiphany of self-revelation in Sneedville in the 1960s. One reporter writes, "Nowadays, a Hancock County resident who can claim to be a Melungeon or a kinsman to a Melungeon is quick to admit it" (Peters 1970). Another article contends that "it has been only in recent years that the Melungeons have begun to admit outsiders to their circle and legends" (Mediterranean Scholar 1970). John Welton, director of the drama, appears in articles with slightly modified versions of his take on the surge of Melungeon pride during the play: "Gradually, some of the workmen came to us and, with a certain pride in their voices, told us that they had Melungeon blood. It was as if 'Walk Toward the Sunset' made it acceptable — maybe even desirable — to be Melungeons" (quoted in Schroeder 1991).

Community Reception

Despite media conjecture on Melungeon pride — and the alleged Melungeon sightings by the media — evidence for Melungeon self-identification tends to be sketchy. In fact most media quotes by a real Melungeon hail from Claude Collins, a community member central to the development of the drama and a well-established leader and businessman in Hancock County. Collins repeats to reporters, "I'm a Melungeon and I'm proud of it," and there is his oft-cited remark: "At one time people just didn't mention the word 'Melungeon,' but today everybody wants to be one" (Winkler 2004, 202; Interview by author). While Collins was front and center in his support, others in the community had markedly different reactions to the production of the Melungeon drama and to the presumed Melungeon heritage that inundated the community and individuals' lives in the aftermath of the drama.

According to those I interviewed, community reactions to the play varied greatly. A few individuals I interviewed participated in the play in some way. As mentioned earlier Claude Collins became integral in the production of the play and remembers its impact in optimistic terms. At one point he even led bus tours through Vardy Valley to offer tourists the opportunity to see Melungeons. Collins remembers with some humor that this was a short-lived venture, as residents grew resentful about the invasion into their private lives. Wayne Winkler reflects on the sensitivity that existed with Claude Collins's bus tours:

Claude Collins ran afoul of some people leading bus tours through Vardy Valley. And what he was doing was showing them the mission and different places. People got the idea he was saying, now, there's a Melungeon, there's a Melungeon. And they didn't like that. A lot of people went on their own too, so, in a given week, Claude might have gone up there with 1 or 2 bus tours, but there'd be a couple dozen people going on their own. So everybody got mad at Claude, you know, and some people would pull up in somebody's driveway, say, [and ask] where can I find some Melungeons, you know. So, yeah some people got irate about that but, you know. . . . People were interested, and Claude was just trying to feed that interest a little bit.

Playing the First Melungeons

Several individuals interviewed in Hancock County expressed their disapproval of the play at the time. Interestingly this displeasure is remembered entirely on the basis of socioeconomic class and issues of representation. The media portrayals of more exotic Melungeon *origins* seemed secondary and even irrelevant to many with whom I spoke. The general sense among respondents was that these ideas were merely part of the overall media hype related to the drama. As one individual recalls, "There were some folks in town that didn't particularly like the idea that we were having the play, because it was a put down, they felt like, on the county, to portray the poor Melungeon people and, basically, to make them look like they were just . . . well, they were very poor." Another woman points out that she was not allowed to see the play as a young person, because her mother felt like people in the community were all going to be depicted as barefoot and dirty. One of the staunchest critics of the play that I interviewed claims that the organizers solicited the poorest local people to hang around the amphitheater to create a more authentic environment:

They had hired these same people to pass out the brochure and to walk around with their feet dirty. Everything they did, was really just to embarrass. . . . Everybody was really upset. I thought the Sheriff was really going to do some damage to them. . . . And I didn't like it either. I think I went a couple times, and you'd go up where the drama site was, they'd have every one of these kids out here, none of them cleaned up, their hair not combed. . . . And they'd get them to wear the kind of clothes they wanted them to. And they were payin' them too. It just put a bad taste in everybody's mouth.

Though I was not able to corroborate the assertion that locals were paid to look poor for outsiders, it is fair to say that representations of Melungeons at the time favored visual images of poverty. And while the notion that poor people were intentionally used as a kind of scenery for tourists may be overstatement, it is certainly true that the media sought an exotic and, at times, unflattering, image of Melungeons. In fact, stereotypical media representations of Melungeons became more problematic for many locals than the play itself: "They were doin' all the publicity they could with channel 6 and channel 10. Every night they would come on, they woulda went up some hollar, would found somebody too sorry to scratch their head, on tv every night. Everybody got tired of that." Only one individual hints at the issue of ethnicity with regard to the play as he sheepishly remembers that the Melungeon characters in the drama darkened their skin for the performance. Responding to my question of whether Melungeons felt on display at all during the play, he replies:

> We did have some people who were objecting to the play. Even the sheriff at the time was objecting, because he felt like . . . he just liked to run everybody out on a rail, because . . . he was harassing everybody come into the county and wanted to see the play. He felt like they were just running the Melungeon folks down. And he certainly didn't like any locals who were involved with it, because they had the makeup on . . . yeah, some of them had to put makeup on and had to play the role . . . because, you know, you had to do those things to be on stage, had to make sure you separated the Melungeons from the white folks, because that's what the play was all about, how they were treated.

Wayne Winkler, who has written extensively about the drama — and saw the play as a young man — offers a more balanced view regarding positive and negative events associated with the drama. When asked about Melungeons being staged outside of the drama, he talks about a scene at the ticket office remembered by many who attended the play:

Well, the big one was, I remember, you can look in Jean Patterson Bible's book, and see the picture of Molly and Lonnie Bowlin. That was really . . . when you came up to the ticket office, they were there, Molly was playing her dulcimer and Lonnie just sat there, but Lonnie is a real swarthy guy. And so, for tourists coming in, it was like, oh, ok, there's a Melungeon. So that's really what it was. There wasn't really all that . . . I think, probably intentionally, they didn't want to have people standing around like, oh, here's a Melungeon for you to look at, because a lot of people were real sensitive about that.

Winkler acknowledges community tension surrounding the drama, including a bomb threat the night before the opening of the play. Winkler also notes that a nonprofit agency constructed the amphitheater in cooperation with a handful of local volunteers. Still Winkler regards the drama as a success in destigmatizing Melungeonness. While this may certainly be the case, one wonders about any genuine value in destigmatizing an identity that existed almost, if not entirely, through media construction.

CHAPTER FOUR

Becoming Melungeon

In the 1990s the Melungeon legend finally became fully peo-
pled — in copious numbers and with a deafening urgency.
A media heyday accompanied the new Melungeon scene,
this time with a movement of real Melungeons behind it.
The 1990s media reporting on Melungeons was unique in
its generation of ideas that were integrally linked with the
very real ways in which self-identified Melungeons began
to express themselves. A synchronicity between the media and the new Melungeons developed; Melungeons gave
voice and presence to media characterizations, and these
characterizations served as a primer for Melungeon identity. From the mid-1990s on, newspaper and magazine articles were no longer the only, or even primary, media venue through which Melungeons were discussed. Melungeon
websites and listservs on the Internet surfaced and grew
exponentially. The Melungeon Heritage Association (MHA)
formed and initiated annual gatherings referred to as Melungeon Unions. All of these things combined to create a
Melungeon movement that heralded a staggering momentum in the mid-1990s.

The following two chapters focus on the new Melungeon
movement, primarily through analysis of an in-depth questionnaire completed by seventy-six respondents. These chapters present a shift in attention from media representations

of Melungeons to social constructions of Melungeon identity vis-à-vis the individuals newly embracing the identity in the 1990s. In the present chapter, I focus on the process of *becoming* Melungeon, with particular interest in how Melungeon descendants come to claim a new ethnic identity in adulthood and why it is meaningful to them.

Brent Kennedy and the Melungeon Movement

The publication of Brent Kennedy's book *The Melungeons* in 1994 catalyzed the Melungeon movement. An administrator with a PhD in communications and a self-identified Melungeon, Kennedy claimed the role of spokesman rather than scholar when he published the book. Kennedy's book is a hybrid of family history, personal memoir, and amateur historical research. Kennedy begins his story with his experiences with the illness sarcoidosis. Learning that the illness was primarily — though not exclusively — a Middle Eastern and Mediterranean disease, Kennedy began to ask questions about his family history. In 1992 he organized the Melungeon Research Committee, a group that eventually disintegrated under the weight of too much speculation about Melungeons with too little evidence.

In the process of his own research, Kennedy developed very specific views on Melungeon origins and evolution. One of his primary assertions involves the idea that Melungeons have Turkish origins. Kennedy's effort in putting it all together reflects this enduring belief:

> I contend that the remnants of Joao ("Juan") Pardo's forts, joined by Portuguese refugees from Santa Elena, and possibly a few stray Dominicans and Jesuits, exiled Moorish French Huguenots, and escaped Acadians, along with Drake's and perhaps other freed Turkish, Moorish, and Iberian captives, survived on these shores, combined forces over the ensuing years, moved to the hinterlands, intermarried with various

Carolina and Virginia Native Americans, and eventually became the reclusive Melungeons. I as strongly contend that the Turkish/Moorish element was at least in the beginning the predominant one, explaining why the probably Turkish self-descriptive term "Melungeon" came to be associated with the various populations regardless of their location. (Kennedy 1994a, 137)

Kennedy continues in his book to provide linguistic and cultural conjecture linking Melungeons to Turks. His singular pursuit of the Turkish connection has taken many forms, including the development of a relationship with Turkish colleagues and officials, dozens of trips to Turkey, and the establishment of a sister-city relationship between Cesme, Turkey, and Wise, Virginia. With his writings and public appearances, Kennedy became an overnight celebrity of sorts. Few media articles that appeared after 1994 failed to mention or quote Kennedy. Media reports on the proud reclamation of identity ballooned with Kennedy's work. As Kennedy entered the scene, media portrayals of Melungeons reintroduced old themes and shifted to untapped territory in the Melungeon legend.

Kennedy's words resonated with thousands of people, and, from the perspective of the public, he was perceived as an immediate expert on all things Melungeon. Kennedy himself admits to being taken by surprise by the interest and enthusiasm. Kennedy proved to be an ideal candidate as the leader of the new Melungeon movement. He is handsome, with striking blue eyes and weathered skin — physical features readily interpreted as exotic in the public eye. Kennedy is articulate, charismatic, and ready and willing to talk. Although he claims modest motives in writing his book, many of his ideas provided seeds that others borrowed and harvested in dramatically different ways.

Maybe Melungeon?

For most individuals staking a claim in the Melungeon movement, becoming Melungeon involves a great deal of ambiguity. Among the most frequently asked questions directed to members of the MHA is an oft-heard one — "Who are the Melungeons?" The MHA describes Melungeons as a multiethnic group of people believed to have some mixture of European, Native American, and African ancestry. Other questions directed to the MHA relate more specifically to individuals' own identity quests. For example another frequently asked question is, "How can I find out if I have Melungeon ancestry?" In response the MHA provides a nuanced answer, indicating a flexibility in self-identification that has become a significant theme in the Melungeon movement. The MHA begins by stating that if an individual has a documented connection to a Melungeon family, they are Melungeon descendants. They then point out the limitations of such documentation, owing to a limited written record pre-1900 and the surplus of Melungeon surnames. They do suggest, however, that there is a strong possibility of Melungeon heritage if one's family includes certain surnames and was listed as nonwhite in past census records. They then moderate this information with a reminder that Melungeons did not begin to self-identify until the mid-1960s. This lack of identification, combined with anemic records, they warn, make it particularly complicated to definitively claim Melungeon heritage.

As is evident in this response and in formal statements made by the MHA and leaders of the movement, Melungeon identity is supple. Self-identification is unrestrained by any attempt at ethnic gatekeeping. The lack of rigid boundaries for Melungeonness accommodates everybody and validates nobody. It is, perhaps, not surprising then that personal intrigue with the exotic nature of the legend alone prevails as the primary entrance point to becoming Melungeon.

Out of seventy-six respondents to a questionnaire (see Appendix 1), the large majority were not born in geographical areas associated with core Melungeon groups. When asked where they were born, individuals cite a wide range of states, with well over half from Tennessee, Virginia, and Ohio. In terms of core Melungeon areas, only two respondents were born in Hancock County, Tennessee; three in Scott County, Virginia; three in Lee County, Virginia; and two in Wise County, Virginia. Of course this does not necessarily mean that all individuals in the Melungeon movement have no connection with core Melungeon areas. In some cases individuals had parents born in Hancock County (or the Virginia counties) who migrated elsewhere but retained strong ties with the area. For example one respondent remembers a childhood with enduring connections to Hancock County despite his family's migration out of Appalachia for jobs: "You know my dad came from Hancock County. So when he and my mom married they moved out to Los Angeles and then Detroit where I was born and that's where I grew up. But we came back here all the time. It's funny, we'd come down the old hillbilly highway, I-75, and sometimes at rest stops, restaurants along the way, I'd see classmates of mine, because the Midwest is full of transplanted hillbillies, so every now and then you'd see somebody that you knew. But we came down frequently."

The large number of respondents born outside of core Melungeon areas, however, does suggest a breach between those newly involved in the Melungeon movement and individuals who grew up in geographical regions associated with historical Melungeons. Among most individuals in my research, Melungeonness was not an organic identity, meaning that individuals simply do not recall being Melungeon before they chose to do so as adults. This is most evident by the fact that, when asked if they consider themselves Melungeon, individuals consistently elaborate on and qualify their responses. A handful of individuals respond with answers like, "I don't know," or use qualifiers, such as "possibly" and "maybe." Most commonly, respondents clarify that they consider themselves Melungeon descendants.

The responses to such a straightforward question of whether or not one considers himself or herself Melungeon illustrate the often confusing, and arbitrary, process by which many come to think of themselves as Melungeon. The question of whether or not individuals consider themselves Melungeon seems to suggest to respondents a kind of definitiveness that makes them uncomfortable and elicits a large number of measured responses. In part this is the result of delineating an identity that is slippery at best, a fact acknowledged constantly among Melungeon descendants at the Unions and on internet discussion lists. Given the nature of the official MHA view, the responses regarding self-identification are understandable.

In one way, qualified identities speak to a hesitancy involved in claiming an identity that has been acquired rather than ascribed. In at least one case, a woman from the Midwest reflects an unusual sensitivity to the potential appropriation of the historical experience of being Melungeon. She reflects: "I may be a descendant of a Melungeon but I did not live the life of someone else who was PERCEIVED as something other than white." For those less prone to this kind of cultural sensitivity, the hesitancy in being fully Melungeon reflects a noncommittal self-identification with which one can deploy, retract, and redefine Melungeon identity at will.

The New Melungeons

The majority of respondents report first hearing the word Melungeon in the 1990s; only a few claim to have heard the term throughout their lives. When asked the context in which they heard the term, nobody specifies being *called* a Melungeon. Those few who heard the term before the 1990s typically heard their family use the term in reference to others, or heard it at school. For example one woman remembers learning about Melungeons in a high school biology class in Kingsport, Tennessee: "We were told they were a strange ethnic group in the mountains." Another young woman born in Ohio who relocated in the western United States recalls hearing her extended family talk about Melungeons when she was a child: "My parents never used the word Melungeon. I heard it first when I was a young teenager in the early 1970s. We visited my grandmother's sisters who still lived in Kentucky and Tennessee and while at the kitchen table, I recall them talking about "Me-lan-gi-a," I cannot remember what they said, but I do recall it was in warning of the Sizemores and another family name to 'stay away from.'"

Those who first heard about Melungeons in the last decade or two discovered them through three main venues: genealogical research, the Internet, and Kennedy's 1994 book. In this vein, hearing about Melungeons is often discussed as a kind of quest, typically involving some kind of genealogical riddle. For example a woman recalls learning about Melungeons while researching her family: "I first heard the word Melungeon while doing my grandfather's side of the family. I was constantly hitting brick walls and as I continued to research, I came across the Melungeons which seemed to include his ancestors. I had started doing some research and was at a family get-together when a cousin said, 'Our family was Melungeon.' I asked questions no one could answer and started to research Melungeons. About a month later my sister and I went to hear Brent Kennedy at the University of Tennessee."

Often genealogical searches take on mystical undertones. A retired amateur genealogist remembers, "I found a book to which I was drawn in a used bookstore in Little Switzerland, North Carolina. My surname was listed in the book." Another woman reveals, "I had an intuition to go to North Carolina. I went to a library in West Jefferson. As soon as my sister and I walked in the librarian said, 'I know why you are here.' She brought out articles on Melungeons."

Media-based introductions to Melungeons are also often relayed as a kind of epiphany. One woman eagerly reflects on her journey: "I was looking for the lyrics for the traditional song, 'Wayfaring Stranger' and I typed it into the yahoo search engine. I ended up at this essay about Melungeons so I kept looking at links and was shocked to find four of the last names in my recent family tree in the lists of common Melungeon names. . . . I looked at related sites for hours until I finally went to bed at three in the morning. It explained a lot of prominent features in my family." More often than not, this kind of transcendence à la the media involves Brent Kennedy. A respondent states, "I was about forty-five years old. I read about Brent Kennedy's book in the newspaper and immediately called the publisher to order a copy for me and had one sent to my sister." When those who identify as Melungeon were asked when they began to think of themselves as Melungeon, respondents regularly invoke Brent Kennedy's name. Many elaborate on their self-discovery vis-à-vis Kennedy's work.

> **Question:** When did you begin to think of yourself as Melungeon?
>
> I have ALWAYS known something was "different" with my family but did not know WHAT until I read *The Melungeons* by Brent Kennedy and recognized these people looked like my family.
>
> The second I read Kennedy's articles! It was like coming home.
>
> When I heard Brent Kennedy speak about ten years ago and I bought his book and found out I was related to him.

Becoming Melungeon

After reading a newspaper item and Dr. Brent Kennedy's TV thing, I had an urge to learn more.

Some of the information in Kennedy's article rang a bell, I don't remember what. It was compelling enough for me to try to find out more.

Shortly after reading Brent's article, I began researching Melungeons on the internet. Within a few weeks, I felt this explained many hitherto unexplained things in my family. We have several Melungeon surnames as well.

It didn't make any difference to me because I never heard anyone talk about it. I just started thinking about it when Dr. Kennedy started talking about it and the publicity it received.

Clearly Kennedy plays a fundamental role in the process of many individuals accessing a Melungeon identity. In large part this seems to relate to Kennedy's all-encompassing approach to Melungeonness. In his talks and writing, Kennedy elasticizes Melungeon identity to the point of anonymity, repeatedly communicating the inclusiveness of the Melungeon movement. Kennedy makes it both easy and appealing to become Melungeon, providing a template for individuals already ensconced in genealogical searches. The adaptable nature of this template allows for—even welcomes—the ambivalence so integral to the process of becoming Melungeon. In the rhetoric of the Melungeon movement, it is never quite possible to fully prove one's Melungeonness; indeed the lack of proof becomes a component of being Melungeon.

This laissez-faire approach to identity does not completely erase measures by which one comes to claim or legitimate Melungeonness. However these measures are not formal, and discussions of them often lead to tension and identity contestations within the movement. Wary of these issues, the MHA includes a strong warning in its overall mission statement that opposes any exclusionary attempts among

Melungeon descendants. In particular the MHA points out that there is not a genetic or genealogical test to being Melungeon. Still, respondents in my research reflect a collective narrative related to identity validation. Not surprisingly the measures by which individuals interpret and legitimate their Melungeonness involve a fluidity that only serves to make Melungeonness more obscure.

Bloodlines

Folk understandings of "blood" and "lines" are prominent in most processes of identity-making and particularly in the case of Melungeons. For example individuals who consider themselves Melungeons commonly borrow the language of blood quantum so familiar in the process of Native American identification. When asked if they identify as Melungeons, respondents often answer in percentages or fractions, such as "100%," "half," "75% sure," and "about one-third to one-half." Less mathematical equations with the same underlying meanings include answers such as "somewhat" and "partly." Respondents also employ the metaphor of blood more directly, such as "I consider I have Melungeon blood" and "I have Melungeon blood through my mother's line." These blood metaphors hint at a rhetoric of purity when considering one's Melungeon identity. For example one respondent wrote, "Grandfather was probably Melungeon therefore I have Melungeon ancestry (probably) but am not 'pure Melungeon.'"

As with other blood metaphors (Sturm 2002), blood quantum among Melungeons is thought of in terms of ancestral references. Among Melungeons genealogy is employed regularly to legitimate one's identity. For example one male writes: "I do not call myself Melungeon but the majority of my lines are of Melungeon descent so I am." Similarly a female respondent states: "I consider some ancestors Melungeon so part of me is Melungeon." Others are more specific

Becoming Melungeon

in referencing their genealogies. One woman explains: "I have one possible Melungeon line known—Goings, whose mother may have been Collins." It is not uncommon for respondents to answer that they do consider themselves Melungeon and then list family names. In one case a respondent well-known among the community as a core Melungeon simply lists her own name in response to the question, "Do you consider yourself Melungeon?"

The issue of genealogy represents an interesting transition in Melungeon identification that paralleled the publication of Kennedy's book. Prior to the book, writers associated historical Melungeons with a handful of surnames. Kennedy, however, expanded this list of names to 137. This expansion offered considerable leeway in making one's own genealogical claims to historical Melungeonness. As Winkler puts it, "With 137 possible names, the odds of finding one of those names in one's individual family tree were pretty good—especially if one lived in or had ancestors from southern Appalachia" (Winkler 2004, 213).

Secrets and Lies

While the majority of respondents self-identify as Melungeon descendants, when asked if their parents identify—or identified—as Melungeon, the overwhelming majority respond that their parents did not and do not. The few who claim that their parents do identify as Melungeon indicate that this self-identification occurred recently—typically as a result of the respondents' own research. For example one woman answers, "After I explained it to them they did." The lack of parental self-identification as Melungeon creates an inherent conflict when one claims a Melungeon identity. Particularly since ancestral linkages are understood to be so important, the lack of ancestral knowledge poses a problem. When stating that their parents did not identify as Melungeon, respondents typically resort to dual strategies as explanation. A common strategy is for respondents to temper answers with provisos that suggest their parents realized they were something other than white but didn't know they were Melungeon. For example respondents commonly suggest that their parents understood themselves as all or part Native American. One woman explains her memory of some kind of eclectic, Native American-Appalachian mix: "My parents never used the word Melungeon; they used hillbilly and 'part Cherokee.'" Still others remember more measured responses by their parents when strangers inquired about ethnicity. One male states: "I am not sure what my mother thought. She almost never talked about her family or origins. If anyone asked 'what she was' she almost always answered, 'What do you think?' Usually, whatever the person said, she agreed with. If a person was unsure, she usually answered Italian or Italian 'throwback' whatever that means."

A second strategy employed by respondents to qualify their parents' lack of Melungeon identity involves references to the popular notion of a conspiracy of secrecy among older Melungeons. When asked if their parents identified as Melungeon, respondents include comments such as "Not when I was at home" and "No, their families never spoke about it." Many responses more explicitly address the idea of a hidden past:

> They took great pains in hiding our ethnicity including moving from the East to West Coast.
>
> Only my mother was Melungeon. She knew, I think, of her ancestors somewhat, however, she never mentioned it to me or my sister.
>
> My dad was three years old when his mother died. She was the one of Melungeon descent and my mother's mother was also but the family hid the fact.

Others elaborate in more detail on the alleged concealment of identity. For example one woman relates: "My mother is not Melungeon. She is of German and recent Native
American descent. That's how she explains my ethnic looks.
My father, well, he still wants to believe in the cover of a
Tuckaho tribe, and I don't really blame him. You grow up
thinking you are one thing and you live your life as one thing
. . . it is hard to change. I honestly can not look at myself
in the mirror and not see the features."

This concept of family secrets is a prominent theme in
the Melungeon movement. Brent Kennedy was the first to
mention the ire he encountered when approaching family
members to talk about Melungeon heritage. One reporter
characterizes Kennedy's entanglement with family history in dramatic form: "What emerged from his crucible of
pain and curiosity was a deep, abiding desire to learn why
his family would never discuss being Melungeon, why his
mother's people were called the 'Black Nashes,' why the
M-word still made many of his contemporaries bristle. . . .
So he went onto Stone Mountain and poked. He went onto
Coeburn Mountain and pried. He alienated family members with questions; some even destroyed photos to prevent him from getting them. Burn in hell, one cousin told
him" (Anthony 1998).

The media perpetuates this idea of a cult of silence to
further mystify Melungeonness. One reporter describes
this phenomenon at First Union: "It was like the chorus of
a song: over and over, First Union attendees talked about
the long code of silence in their families, the warnings
from elders to not ask too many questions, the shame of
their dark-skinned mystery" (Schroeder 1997). Other journalists suggest the idea that not only were family clues to
identity buried, but also the very existence of a lack of information might indicate Melungeonness. For example a
reporter advises: "Look for families that seem to have no

history or one that just does not seem to 'fit'. . . . Often, because the history was lost or hidden, it is only by surname, vague traditions and 'facts' that don't check out that one can make connections back to Melungeons" (Baldwin 1996). A respondent in my research mimics this idea as she describes Melungeons as "a group that has a family history of disassociation with mainstream society at least in some part, somewhere in your family and unique family stories that somehow do not fit."

Few scholars would contest that historically many multiethnic families went to great lengths to cloak or erase any hints of blackness. However responses in my research adopt a folkloric element, as if the very act of identity concealment among early generations serves as a kind of Melungeon litmus test. Alternative options to the notion of genealogical sabotage—that, perhaps, family members simply did not hold any secrets—are rarely, if ever, part of the Melungeon dialogue. Thus secrets tend to become a key criterion for claiming Melungeon identity.

Medicalizing Melungeonness

Increasingly—and intriguingly—testimony to one's Melungeon identity lies with the prevalence of physical traits and medical illnesses. Despite his sweeping rhetoric on the boundless Melungeon family, Kennedy—by virtue of his own story—impacted Melungeon attempts at identity confirmation in significant ways. On the most basic level, he was the first to talk spiritedly about physical traits unique to Melungeons. The most prevalent among these are believed to be polydactylism, and what are referred to as an Anatolian bump, Asian eye fold, and shovel teeth. The following description, borrowed from Nancy Sparks Morrison, provides a thorough overview of these particular physical traits:

Becoming Melungeon

There are some physiological characteristics which are not entirely documented, but seem to be passed on through the lines of some Melungeon descendants. There is a bump on the back of the HEAD of SOME descendants that is located at mid-line just ABOVE the juncture with the neck. It is about the size of half a golf ball or smaller. If you cannot find the bump, check to see if you, like some descendants, including myself, have a ridge, located at the base of the head where it joins the neck, rather than the Anatolian bump. My ridge is quite noticeable. It is larger than anyone else's that I have felt, except my father's. I can lay one finger under it and the ridge is as deep as my finger is thick. Other ridges are smaller. To find a ridge, place your hand at the base of your neck where it joins your shoulders, and on the center line of your spine. Run your fingers straight up your neck toward your head. If you have a ridge, it will stop your fingers from going on up and across your head. People who live in the Anatolian region of Turkey also have this "bump." There is also a ridge on the back of the first four teeth—two front teeth and the ones on either side (upper and lower) of some descendants. If you place your fingernail at the gum line and gently draw (up or down) you can feel it and it makes a slight clicking sound. The back of the teeth also curve outward rather than straight as the descendants of Anglo-Saxon parentage do. Teeth like these are called Asian Shovel Teeth. Many Indian descendants also have this type of teeth. The back of the first four teeth of Northern European descendants are straight and flat. SOME Melungeon descendants have what is called an Asian eye fold. This is rather difficult to describe. At the inner corner of the eye, the upper lid attaches slightly lower than the lower lid. That is to say that it overlaps the bottom lid. If you place your finger just under the inner corner of the eye and gently pull down, a wrinkle will form which makes the fold more visible. Some people call these eyes, "sleepy eyes, dreamy eyes, bedroom eyes." Many Indian descendants also have these kinds of eyes. Some families may have members with fairly dark skin who suffer with vitiligo, a loss of pigmentation, leaving the skin blotched with white patches. Some descendants have had six fingers or toes. There is a family of people in Turkey whose surname translated into English is "Six Fingered Ones."

Although Morrison has been sidelined somewhat by the MHA for her emphasis on Melungeon physiology and illness, her outline of Melungeon characteristics is consistent with what Kennedy and others discuss at public gatherings. Moreover this notion of Melungeon traits predominates among Melungeon descendants as part of their social construction of identity. For example, when asked to describe themselves, respondents commonly list variations on what are presumed to be Melungeon physical traits, such as "Asian shovel teeth," "shovel-shaped incisors," "ridge on the back of my head," "eyes with overlapping folds," and "Asiatic eyes." When asked to describe Melungeons, well over half of all respondents list one or more of these physical traits.

Perhaps more significant than physical characteristics, however, is Kennedy's personal story about his life-threatening illness. When Kennedy was forty-five, he became bedridden with a disease eventually diagnosed as sarcoidosis and familial Mediterranean fever (FMF). His illness was traumatic in its intensity and mystery. Genetically based diseases common among Middle Eastern and Mediterranean populations, sarcoidosis and FMF were not on the diagnostic radar for most rural Appalachian doctors treating a largely Scots-Irish population. Following years of crippling bouts of illness, Kennedy finally received a correct diagnosis and treatment from an Atlanta physician. His illness and recovery served as an epiphany for him as he pondered the hereditary nature of these diseases and his own long-held questions about his family's dark physical features. In one article, Kennedy reflects: "I thought I was dead, and I lived. . . . So my perspective on life changed. I had a lot of questions that needed answering, and I set out to answer them." These included "questions such as why his brother looked like Saddam Hussein. Why his mother's family was called the Black Nashes. . . . Why as a girl, his mother wasn't allowed to play in the sun without full cover to keep her skin from turning even darker. And most of all, why his family refused to answer any of these questions" (Schroeder 1997).

Kennedy's story prompted several new, interrelated themes in media portrayals of Melungeons. Kennedy's struggle with sarcoidosis and FMF, in the context of his proclamation of Melungeon heritage, offered a novel direction for journalists to expand upon the legendary Melungeons. With Kennedy the media constructs the illusion of a more tangible Melungeon — one that can be defined in physiological, medical, and genetic terms. In the media Kennedy embodies sarcoidosis and FMF, and these diseases became equated with Melungeon descent.

For much of the Melungeon movement, Kennedy's exotic illness, combined with his speculation about his family's mixed race heritage, allots him credentials as a real Melungeon. Sensitive to the problematic nature of identity via Melungeon illnesses, the MHA includes a cautionary statement under "Misconceptions." The caption reads, "Does the Bump on my Head Mean I'm a Melungeon?" followed by an ardent explanation:

Much has been made, in the press and on the Internet, about so-called "Melungeon diseases," or physical characteristics such as "shovel teeth" or "Anatolian ridges" on the base of the skull. Some reporters and writers have widely misinterpreted these traits as indicators of Melungeon ancestry. Many people involved with Melungeon research have been approached by someone who has said, "Feel the back of my head—am I a Melungeon?" Others, upon learning of one's Melungeon heritage, will ask, "What is that disease you guys have?" Although these characteristics are significant in each individual's family and genetic history, they do not necessarily represent Melungeon ancestry. The diseases most widely reported as relating to Melungeons include Familial Mediterranean Fever, Thallasemia, and several other ailments. The only real significance of these diseases in relation to Melungeons is that some people of Melungeon descent have been diagnosed with these diseases, many of which tend to affect people of Mediterranean ancestry, and are relatively rare among the Anglo-Saxon or Celtic people of Appalachia. Those who have one of these diseases have reason to believe that someone in their ancestry had an ethnic disposition to this particular disease. However, it is a mistake to assume this ailment, in and of itself, is an indication that one is a Melungeon. Relatively few people of Melungeon descent have these diseases, but unfortunately several reports have focused on the disease issue to the point where many believe that having one of these diseases is a primary indication of Melungeon ancestry, or that all Melungeons are afflicted. Shovel teeth, bumps on the back of the head, polydactylism (extra fingers), and other characteristics have likewise been often misrepresented as being "Melungeon" traits. Actually, "shovel teeth" are found among Native Americans and people from Central Asia. They are not, however, common among Europeans, so there is certainly significance to those who believe themselves of purely European ancestry. The same with the head bumps, which are also indicators of at least one Central European forebear. Many Melungeons have these traits, others do not. Melungeons are an ethnic mix, and each family and individual receives different genetic markers from their various ancestors. These physical characteristics are not insignificant. They demonstrate that many "White" Americans had ancestors who were NOT "White" in the generally accepted sense of the word. Again, however, these traits do not necessarily indicate Melungeon ancestry. Brent Kennedy and others first began talking about these characteristics and their significance over a decade ago, and many of those who have reported on his work come up with the same mistaken interpretation—that these are "Melungeon" traits. Most recently, the History Channel led off a report on Melungeons with talk of shovel teeth. Another frequent query posted to the Melungeon Heritage Association concerns genetic testing to determine Melungeon ancestry. Genetic testing cannot establish a Melungeon heritage because the Melungeons are of mixed ethnic ancestry, and all of us show different results on various tests. The tests DO show some interesting things about our individual families, but don't tell us much about Melungeons as a whole.

Despite the best efforts of the MHA to quell the amplification of medical issues in the Melungeon discourse, the group regularly features educational sessions during the Unions, such as "Tracking Melungeons Medical Conditions." The reality is that understandings of physiology and illness are significant elements in many individuals' social construction of a Melungeon identity. Indeed a number of individuals responding to my questionnaire answer the question of when they began to think of themselves as Melungeons with references to physiological symptoms. One woman answers: "When I developed pulmonary fibrous [sic] of the lungs with no known cause." Another respondent claims a similar discovery related to presumed Melungeon physiology: "When I discovered the Anatolian knot on my head, shown to me by Brent Kennedy." Others claim a Melungeon identity based on diagnoses of FMF or a range of varying symptoms they identify as FMF. Sporadic references to physiology also surface in responses to other questions. When asked if her parents identified as Melungeon, one amateur genealogist wrote: "Not until I was diagnosed with familial Mediterranean fever did my dad consider himself Melungeon."

In a more in-depth exploration of beliefs about Melungeon identity vis-à-vis illness, my research included questions aimed to elicit folk ideologies of illness among those who believe they suffer from a Melungeon-related illness.[1] When asked if they suffer from, or think they suffer from, a Melungeon-related illness, half of the overall respondents report an illness or multiple illnesses. The problems listed vary widely, including sinus problems, obesity, heart problems, diabetes, anemia, manic depression, and food allergies. It is clear that what Melungeon descendants understand as a Melungeon-related illness covers a vast range and that a large number of Melungeon descendants have a tendency to think of Melungeon identity and illness as interlinked.

Among respondents listing illnesses, most made specific reference to illnesses perceived widely as Melungeon-based, particularly FMF. One individual mentions polydactylism, and one person reports having sarcoidosis; however, the majority either use the label "familial Mediterranean fever," or cite joint pain and/or fibromyalgia with reference to FMF. Within this group—without exception—individuals describe their illnesses as genetically based. The most common symptoms listed are joint pain, fatigue and fevers. When asked if they had consulted a doctor and how the doctor responded, a small number of individuals claim an official diagnosis by their physician. In most cases the medical community does not issue many formal diagnoses of FMF. The lack of diagnoses is typically explained by respondents as ignorance on the physician's part (many times echoing

Becoming Melungeon

Brent Kennedy's story that his years of misdiagnosis result-ed from ignorance among doctors about multiethnic Ap-palachians). For example one woman complains that her doctor refuses to treat her self-diagnosed FMF: "The doc-tor I consulted w/ does not believe in the origin of Melun-geons and wouldn't treat me—because of insurance, I can't see the doctor who is working w/ FMF in my area." Anoth-er respondent offers a similar commentary: "I asked to be tested for FMF but the doctor refused. She said, 'But you have never had peritonitis.' I said, 'But my sister, mother and aunt have had it.' She still wouldn't order the test." In a similar vein a male recalls his doctor's skepticism: "Most doctors told me I had rheumatory arthritis even though ex-tensive tests revealed no trace of arthritis in my body. My last doctor tested me for over a month and eliminated ev-erything but FMF. Told me he had never come across FMF before and prescribed colchicine before my tests were com-pleted, just to be safe." Another woman responds that a number of doctors "cannot pinpoint the reason . . . there-fore do not prescribe meds." Similarly, a woman comments that her doctor just "runs tests and shakes his head." Sever-al respondents were prescribed antidepressants, with var-ied responses. A couple of individuals felt insulted and did not take the medication, while others understood depres-sion to be a symptom of their larger illness.

Others reveal that their doctors did not formally diag-nose them but made vague allusions that the patients in-terpreted as affirming a Mediterranean identity. For exam-ple one woman asserts that her doctor advised a special diet and over-the-counter pills for pain, but noted to the patient that "You do look different from other people." An-other untreated woman notes: "Doctors kept asking me if I had Mediterranean blood because they could not give an accurate diagnosis."

The fact that FMF captures the imagination of many

Melungeon descendants is likely explained by the fact that folk understandings of FMF's symptoms mimic more commonly identified illnesses, such as fibromyalgia, depression, anxiety, and chronic fatigue syndrome. It is not uncommon for Melungeons who claim to suffer from FMF to express a sense of relief in learning about the illness, particularly those who suffer vague symptoms that have marginal legitimacy within the biomedical community. The interpretation of FMF symptomatology among Melungeons involves a flexibility that accommodates a range of physical complaints, however vague they may be. At the same time the establishment of FMF as an illness one has—even when self-diagnosed—communicates legitimacy in one's identification as Melungeon.

The only realm that provides an even greater sense of validation of Melungeon descent is DNA testing. Discussions of DNA testing came to the fore among Melungeons in 2000 as the result of a study conducted by Kevin Jones, a biologist at the University of Virginia at Wise. Sampling a population of core Melungeons selected, in part, by Brent Kennedy, the study revealed findings that were consistent with an earlier DNA study by Pollitzer and Brown (1969) —Melungeon descendants reflect a tri-racial group that is predominantly European with some African American and Native American ancestry.[2] Jones's study received mixed reactions among contemporary Melungeons and in the media. Kennedy publically interprets the results of the study in ways that coincide with his well-established views. He professes that the DNA results simply reveal the enormous variation within European ancestry. Journalists reflect a more cautious reading, primarily offered by Kevin Jones. One writer reports:

> The DNA data told people who felt a deep connection to American Indians that their ancestors were mostly white. It informed

a lot of blonde-haired, blue-eyed people that at least some of their forebears were black. And it delivered a particularly cruel message to Kennedy: That his deeply cherished sense of himself and his community might never be proved, and the origins of the rare genetic disease that nearly killed him might never be known. What did it all mean? "Whatever you want it to," Jones told the audience. "If you were hoping for a DNA sequence that says you're Melungeon, forget it." (McGowan 2003)

In most ways, the lack of DNA confirmation is not a game-changer for Melungeon descendants. Indeed DNA evidence would be at odds with the elasticity of Melungeon identification. The broader process of medicalization vis-à-vis physiology and illness leaves much greater room for interpretation. With illness individuals can use physical markers or symptoms to solidify their identity choice and enhance their perceived biological kinships in a biomedical culture that increasingly normalizes the medicalization of identity (Finkler 2001).

Heritage and History

Any discussion of the process of becoming Melungeon is driven by a more central question of why one wants to be Melungeon. Since for most in the Melungeon movement, the identity is acquired rather than ascribed, becoming Melungeon is a matter of choice. The fact that so many individuals have chosen to be Melungeon suggests a payoff of some kind. In part being Melungeon might offer an explanation for unknowns in one's family or medical history. On a broader level being Melungeon appears to give individuals a sense of rootedness, meaning, and community. Waters (1990) suggests that choosing a white ethnicity provides a potent combination of belonging to a group while maintaining one's individuality through distinction as a special (i.e., nonwhite) person. Among Melungeon descendants this sense of belonging is key. Respondents understand meanings of Melungeonness in personal terms, viewing Melungeon identity in relation to their own sense of rootedness. For many, such romantic meanings of Melungeonness provide a sense of relief or catharsis. One respondent suggests that being Melungeon is equivalent to "peace of mind." This sense of belonging and/or finding meaning and comfort in one's life is particularly evident among respondents when asked how learning about Melungeons changed the way one thinks about himself or herself:

> I have received traditions, values and beliefs from my mother based on her Melungeon heritage.
>
> I feel more satisfied knowing my true roots and having an explanation of my different looks.
>
> I wear a gold necklace with a plate that says "Melungeon." I have a T-shirt with a picture of my father, mother, brothers and sister with "Melungeon and Proud." I am special and have tight ties.
>
> I know if my Indian part of my background don't accept me, I fit in and this group accepts me with open arms.
>
> I consider myself as a part of an American, mixed race culture now, instead of a lone individual.
>
> I knew without a shadow of doubt the reasons for my confusion and insecurity of my life experience.
>
> I feel stronger that I overcame my mother's poverty and humble past.
>
> I feel stronger. I think about the women in my family and all they had to contend with, yet they raised families and lived with more obvious racial obstacles. I feel validated in singing gospel, soul and blues; I have a right.

Becoming Melungeon is a journey with significant personal rewards for most individuals today. Like other white ethnics (Waters 1990), Melungeon descendants gain a strong sense of community, heritage, and meaning through the process.

Melungeonness brings personal rewards for most who embrace the identity. At the same time claims to Melungeon identity are costless on an individual basis (Waters 1990). Becoming Melungeon is a pliable and noncommittal process. Definitive Melungeon markers are nonexistent, and folk measures of identity validation involve creative interpretation. Indeed the ambiguity involved in defining Melungeonness becomes an integral part of the essence of being Melungeon. For example when asked what it means to be Melungeon, respondents answer with comments like, "Let's let it define itself," and "there are no real boundaries to say what we are." Becoming Melungeon is reflective of what Gallagher (2003) terms an "ethnic grazing." As will be discussed in depth in the next chapter, this casual grazing involves an unspoken hierarchy of ethnic preference that reveals a great deal about contemporary racial politics.

CHAPTER FIVE

The Mediterranean Mystique

For many Melungeon descendants the 2002 DNA studies promised a definitiveness in identifying Melungeons as an ethnic group. A great deal of anticipation led up to Kevin Jones's report at the Melungeon Union, and, for most attendees, the results were anticlimactic at best. Broadly speaking, some individuals disliked any proof of African American heritage. Following Jones's announcement, the media focuses on his recounting of death threats by those loathe to confirm any semblance of blackness. There is little doubt that the DNA studies ignited an element of the explicit racist passions so grounded in the South's legacy. Yet reactions to the DNA studies cannot be simplified as temporarily resurrected Jim Crow racism. Certainly for every death threat made to Kevin Jones, there were dozens of Melungeon descendants eager to communicate their delight with the idea of a multiethnic identity. These responses of delight and denial are at the crux of the overall point that the Melungeon movement is inextricably linked with racial politics in the contemporary United States. Melungeon commentators have simply not addressed in any depth the relationship between the current Melungeon movement and contemporary constructions of race. The racial politics involved in the hierarchy of identity attainment among Melungeon descendants prevail as the white elephant in the room. In this chapter I address how the contemporary articulation of Melungeon identity resonates with larger racial and cultural politics in the United States.

Almost Indian

Though they represent a distinct minority, a small group of Melungeon descendants advocate for recognition as indigenous people. In a public hearing with the Tennessee Commission on Indian Affairs in 1999, approximately a dozen Melungeons gathered to discuss formal criteria for indigenous status. Politically sanctioned Native American tribes disregard politically active Melungeons as "dead spirits" and "wannabes." Very few of those who identify themselves as Melungeons in Tennessee have documentation of Native American ancestry. They angrily dismiss official criteria as prejudicial to those mixed-blood people who severed connections to Native American ancestry as a result of the westward removal of Native Americans in the 1830s. Melungeon activists also argue that, historically, Melungeons intentionally distanced themselves from Native American ancestors to more successfully assimilate to Anglo Appalachia. The strategic arrangement of genealogies throughout Melungeon history, coupled with the prolific miscegenation between Melungeons and white Appalachians, results in complexities not easily reconciled with state and federal criteria for Native American recognition.

In public discussion surrounding official legitimation, Native American ethnic identity is essentialized through impressive visual displays of Mohawks, headdresses, and silver and turquoise jewelry. Beyond visual dynamics, Melungeon activists struggle for legitimation through nebulous emotional claims to Indianness. One Melungeon, speaking at the Tennessee Commission, remembers growing up knowing he was a little darker than others in a family that honored "staying to ourselves." At the same time he recalls an affection for playing Indian, a source of conflict for his father who admonished him: "I'm going to prove you're Portugee, not Indian." Others describe similar compulsions to play Indian as children. A young woman, for example, remembers being sent home from school to scrub what her teacher thought were her dirty knees and tearfully describes her attraction to Indian things as "just like part of my soul." Another young man proudly acknowledges his affinity for dating Indian women exclusively (despite the fact, he points out, that white girls are always chasing him). Also evident is the tendency to couch claims to Indian heritage in terms of a respect for elders and family. When discussing their Indianness, respondents speak in mystical terms of a creator and claim a reverence for the earth. They also discuss active participation in sweat lodges and powwows.

In contrast to references to "blacks" and the "white man," most Melungeon activists use "my people" and "our people" when talking about Native Americans. For example one Melungeon speaking at the Commission claims that "we Indians are the only people treated worse than the blacks." Another accuses Melungeons of "playing the white man's game better than he does."

A distinct pride frames almost all declarations of heritage among Melungeon activists, a pride that is reflected most commonly by disclaimers to wanting "the card," the documentation that officially recognizes Native Americans. The card represents a central theme in public discussion on native recognition, typically portrayed as an insignificant by-product, secondary to dignity and recognition. In the words of one Melungeon: "We don't want to be a tribe. We don't want money. We are working people who want dignity. We are not wannabes. We just wannabe left alone." Or, in the more indignant words of another Melungeon, "We don't want your stinkin' card. We don't want your money.

We just want recognition, to be counted, for our children and grandchildren."

Those who acknowledge a desire for the card do so with a similar sense of pride and, in some cases, redemption. An older Melungeon, sporting Mohawk and earrings, stated his desire for the card to "legally" dance in Indian pow-wows. With much more dramatic flair, another Melungeon dancer speaks about his desire for the card as a passport to recognition by the full-bloods who allegedly taunt him by suggesting that he wear duck rather than eagle feathers. In true Southern style he explains what he would do with the card: "When challenged by full-bloods, I can pull out that card and say, 'What ya think of that bro?' Hell, I grew up knowing more about Native American culture than most Native Americans. 'I got your card, cuz.'"

Interviews with Melungeon activists are a telling example of the distortion of ethnic identity when it is packaged for political expediency. Such distortions promote ethnic dissension between Melungeons and federally recognized Native American tribes whose members perceive Melungeons as cheaply appropriating a long-embattled identity. The distortion of ethnicity is also problematic for many Melungeons who do not express interest in status as Native Americans and are uncomfortable with the diversion from a mixed ethnic identity. Indeed the MHA and participants in the Melungeon Unions do not express collective interest in political legitimation as native peoples, and the issue of recognition does not enter the discourse at Union gatherings. In fact for the most part Melungeon descendants participating in my questionnaire reflect a savvy appreciation of the politics of federal recognition. Similar to activists, many respondents reflect the same kind of defensive pride in not being formally recognized as Native American. When asked their opinions about Melungeons being officially recognized as Native Americans, responses were largely negative:

DUMB move. Will never happen. The government won't. The Indians would be in uproar (federally recognized and otherwise) if they did. A few individuals may make this decision for themselves according to their lines but forget federal recognition. My husband—in black and white—is related to Cherokee chiefs and has attempted to join federally recognized Cherokees. You can't basically do it if you are over 18.

Not necessary but could probably qualify to be recognized.

I don't think we should be because being Native American is just one part of all our many parts that make us whole.

It is only part of the heritage and I am very happy with who I am (Indian) and don't need the government to recognize us.

I think Melungeons are much more, have more ethnic strains than just Native American, unless you mean original settlers in America.

Absolutely not. There is NO basis of which to do this. I have been aware of ALL studies ever made—none support this, although I agree Melungeons were likely here very early and mixed with Native Americans, etc.

Despite what tends to be a defensive position about formal recognition as Native Americans, Melungeon descendants are enthusiastic about claiming Native American heritage as a part of their overall identity. When prompted, Melungeon descendants perceive Native American characteristics in idealized ways. For example when asked to list Native American traits, characterizations include: spiritual, nonmaterialistic, proud, noble, and stoic. In fact, a mere three individuals mention anything remotely negative, including alcohol problems or lack of education and motivation. Fascination with Indianness in the United States is nothing new, and Melungeons are no exception to the overall trend to romanticize Native Americans (Bird 1996; Deloria 1998; Garroutte 2003). What is more telling are the distinctions individuals draw when listing Native American,

African American, Melungeon, and European traits. Considerable overlap exists between respondents' perceptions of Native American and Melungeon traits. Melungeon descendants identify with what they understand to be Native American, and that they view Melungeons, in general, to be Native American–esque in nature.

Barely Black

In terms of an identity hierarchy among Melungeon descendants, blackness sits at the bottom of the echelon. In contrast to the inventory of Native American traits, respondents' overview of African American traits reflects a more mixed assessment. In general respondents provide an assortment of answers that range from odd to insulting. These include such depictions as: aggressive, social, boisterous, sensual, able to handle heat, musically inclined, angry, poorly educated, loud, insecure, shiftless, disheartened, hypertensive, angry, defensive, rude, hurtful, and agile-bodied. In almost direct contrast to descriptions of Native Americans, only a few individuals offer more complimentary portrayals, writing that African Americans are sensitive, accepting, hard-working, spiritual, loving, and supportive of strong family ties. Among many Melungeon descendants, blackness denotes largely negative associations; it is, perhaps, not surprising then that the traits listed for African Americans did not correspond with those for Melungeons.

As discussed earlier, respondents refer to ethnicity but few list specific ethnic groups when asked, "What does it mean to be Melungeon?" and "How would you describe Melungeons to future generations?" Among those who do list specific ethnicities, individuals much more commonly include Native American, European, and Mediterranean than African American. In most cases claims to any remnant of blackness are conspicuously absent. While respondents explicitly refer to a Native American or Mediterranean heritage, few describe black ancestry in their characterizations of what it means to be Melungeon. For example one woman describes Melungeons as "of mixed white, Indian and other blood." A male respondent acknowledges that Melungeons represent a mixed race but points out that the mixture is "mostly white." Another male concedes that being Melungeon means "one has dark (but not black) skin." In a similar vein, when asked where they think Melungeons come from, respondents rarely mention an African American or sub-Saharan African connection; if they do, it is typically preceded by a "maybe" or "possibly."

Those who refer to black or African identity make a point to minimize or qualify it. For example one woman speaks to her mother about being of white, black, and American Indian descent. To allay her mother's surprise about the notion of black ancestry, she creates as much distance as possible between her own family and what she terms her black "GGGGG . . . Grandfather."

Even when individuals appear more comfortable discussing black heritage as part of Melungeon identity in general, they are far less likely to claim blackness when discussing their individual ancestries. For example one woman explains potential ethnic amalgamations among Melungeons while pointing out the individual nature of self-identification: "I believe Melungeons to be mixed race people, some white/black, some white/Native American, Native American/black, etc. It depends on the particular string of family." Another woman writes: "I have gone away from just 'MELUNGEON.' My lines appear to have a strong influx of Mediterranean and more Indian."

While it is not particularly illogical to suggest different variations in the ethnicity of Melungeonness, it is fair to question to what extent the combinatory approach to ancestry provides a convenient loophole for one's individual identity claims. When asked how friends and family members reacted to being told about a possible Melungeon ancestry, most respondents report confronting shock, denial, and lack of interest. In general, however, this question tends to elicit more explicit negative reactions to blackness:

Question: Have you talked to your family or friends about being Melungeon? What did you say? What was their reaction?

They don't like to admit any "black descent."

Most said, "You look too far" and I would find a "nigger in the woodpile."

Yes, our ancestors were listed as "C" in 1820 census records, then in later records as "W." One sister was very upset and thought it meant "colored as in Negroid."

I called a cousin one time and she said, "We never had much to do with them. Aunt Grace married a nigger you know."

My mom first laughed because she immediately said, "I married a black man!" My dad was shocked about what I had found and he basically denied although he has all of the characteristics.

My father does not care; he says he is part Cherokee. My mother is dead; she often giggled at the fact her family hid black blood from way, way back.

My parents were not very receptive at first. My father is not willing to accept his own Native American heritage. My mother accepts her Native American heritage and has finally (in the last month) talked about possible African American heritage.

Interviews with Melungeon descendants reflect a similar resistance to African American identity, sometimes including explicitly derogatory and racist remarks, or good-humored dismissals. In general, however, a disassociation from blackness becomes most apparent when individuals discuss their genealogies. People consistently refer to blacks as "they" and "them," rather than "us" and "we." While individuals often appropriate perceived symbols of Indianness or Mediterranean identity, few attempt any kind of symbolic blackness. Only one respondent reflected on

The Mediterranean Mystique

any enthusiasm about becoming aware of his black heritage: "At twelve years old, they say, you're a mix of all these things. This was 1968. James Brown had just put out Say Out Loud, I'm Black and I'm Proud. And I grew up in Detroit. Hey, part black, cool. James is singing to me too. You know, James Brown's all over the radio. Anyway, it wasn't any big deal to me. Only as I got older did I realize, this is what it meant to people a generation or 2 ago."

The overall disregard for blackness does not, necessarily, suggest that Melungeon descendants are unique in their understandings of and attitudes toward race in the United States — nor do Melungeons necessarily reflect more racist ideas than the general population. Indeed the opposition to blackness among Melungeon descendants may well represent a more gentle version of the largely implicit kind of racist discrimination that exists in the United States in general. Still it is appropriate to acknowledge that, among many in the Melungeon movement, the perception of a multiethnic identity on an individual level tends to disavow blackness. This is significant in that, as a collective group, the MHA and Melungeon descendants showcase Melungeon identity as a copasetic multiethnicity that presupposes a non-racialized identity. The problem is that this broad multicultural stance ignores underlying racial discriminations that endure, yet become invisible in the Melungeon rhetoric.

Not Quite White

Although Melungeon descendants express discomfort with blackness, they are also not entirely at ease with whiteness. When asked how others labeled themselves and their families when they were growing up, respondents most commonly respond with "white." However those same individuals consistently mitigate their answers — and, perhaps, their whiteness — with further comments. These qualifications most often include an acknowledgment of some kind of ethnic marking identified by themselves or others, despite being labeled as white:

> **Question:** How did others label you and your family when you were growing up?
>
> Scotch-Irish, English — despite my dark skin, hair, eyes, etc.
>
> We were considered white — my mother always said her family was Welsh and that's where we got the dark skin, hair and eyes.
>
> White, from a very prominent family, but I was described as being "dark as a berry."
>
> Whites, although we had dark skin. One sister was called "blackie."
>
> White, but once in a movie theater, a little brother of a boy we knew asked if my sister and I were colored.

Similar qualifications are made among those who do not claim to have been labeled at all. One woman comments, "We were not labeled but I detected general disassociation with both myself and especially my mother who had very dark olive skin (I have light olive skin) and dark hair." Another woman states, "I do not feel like we were labeled, but looking back, I am sure whites had a different opinion of my colorful family."

Most respondents who list multiple ethnicities when asked how others labeled them growing up, answer with "Native American" and "white." Among those who claim multiple identities, only three include "black" or "African American" as one of their identities, and only one of those listing "black" did not also include "white" as part of their mixed ethnicity. Other labels include Black Dutch, Black Irish, Mexican, Latino, Spanish, Italian, Greek, Gypsy, Jewish, Japanese, Chinese, Moorish, and Arab. Many respondents remember a sort of grab-bag of ethnic labels that generally acknowledge their presumed physical differences. One woman, for example, recalls at length:

The Mediterranean Mystique

As a child I felt I did not belong as I looked very different in relation to my parents. I was teased abut being either Mexican, Spanish or Indian due to my dark features and prominent nose. Children sometimes would not let me play with them or were told by their parents they could not associate with me. My parents told me that was ridiculous as I was clearly Black Irish, Black Welsch, Black German, etc. My parents looked Caucasian with the exception of my father's black hair and gray eyes which is a Melungeon trait. I clearly stood out. I knew that I was different from a very young age and it was very confusing. When we first moved to California and my parents were busy moving into our home, I was alone with the real estate agent. I was five years at the time. I still recall him asking me where I got my big black eyes and dark hair. I told him I was from Egypt! (I have no idea where that came from.) When my parents found out I was severely punished and made to tell him I was Irish. The term Black Irish, Black Welsch, etc. was a term used to hide Melungeon-Native American mulatto identities in order to protect against discrimination and enslavement or worse, being imprisoned.

Only one respondent claims being labeled "Melungeon." Five respondents recall some kind of class-based label, such as "hillbilly," "poor," "ridgerunner," and "white trash." Other responses are interesting as they manage to evade the question altogether with answers, such as: "American," "normal," "no different from themselves," and "as who they were." These answers coincide with a larger sense of resistance to labels common among contemporary Melungeons, likely owing to the rhetoric among the movement of transcending ethnic labels altogether.

Standing Up and Being Counted: The 2000 Census

As is evident above, many individuals express some notion that they and/or their families perceive themselves or were perceived by others as "different" than white. Even when they recognize being labeled as white, individuals often elaborate on their answers to suggest they did not view themselves, and may not have been viewed by others, as fully white. When asked if they completed the 2000 Census, the vast majority respond that they did. When asked what ethnic category or categories they chose, most respondents report identifying as white on the census. Interestingly many individuals who report being white on the census do not acknowledge being labeled white growing up. This contrast suggests that individuals categorize their identities far more loosely when responding informally. However in terms of a more formal self-identification on the census, respondents tend to "whiten" considerably.

The other interesting dynamic with regard to the census relates to the large number of individuals who chose more than one racial or ethnic category. For the first time the 2000 census allowed individuals to self-identify as more than one race or ethnicity. Most respondents who chose multiple categories selected "white" and "Native American," often writing in "Melungeon" in the "other" category. When asked if their self-designation in the 2000 census differed from their choice in the previous census, the vast majority of respondents who claimed multiple identities report that they *did* change their race options. When asked why, responses fall into two categories—those who report discovering or finding their heritage and those who comment that they had the option to choose something other than white for the first time.

Only one respondent chose "African American" as their sole racial category in the 2000 census. This was a designation she had always marked on the census. Two others include "African American" in their multiple identity choices, one of whom had changed her racial identifier in the 2000 census from solely "African American" to "Melungeon, white, black, multiethnic." She explains that she made the change as a result of her increasing sense of multiethnic identity as opposed to being labeled "very light skinned black."

Ethnic and racial designations on the 2000 census became a significant topic of debate for Melungeon descendants in Internet discussions. A great deal of acrimony surrounds whether or not to fill out the census, a number of individuals revealing a distrust of any official attempt to categorize them. Often this distrust is discussed in reference to the past when historical Melungeons were understood as nonwhite and disenfranchised as a result. Individuals debating on the Internet how to fill out the 2000 census commonly invoke this historical backdrop. For example one woman casually remarks: "You know it was poignant and very interesting when I told my husband we need to put Melungeon on the census that he said 'then they will know where to come after us' . . . isn't that funny (not funny ha ha) that after all these generations that was the first thing off the top of his head?. . . Man!! this just might be a people that have a reason to feel a bit nervous! . . . and picked on." Another woman claims a firsthand encounter with discrimination in an interaction with a 2000 census taker: "We were 'accosted' this afternoon by a government census taker, who insisted on knowing what race we were. My husband answered 'American.' She got upset and repeated the question. I began to educate her on my Melungeon heritage, which I am trying to prove. She shook her head in dismay. So where and when will it stop.?? It SHOULD stop with government workers, but it won't. I do not know what she entered in the blank, but probably Caucasian only because I am blonde, out of a bottle."

While many Melungeon descendants are reluctant to fill out the census based on what they perceive as ancestral discrimination, others proudly explain their process of entering a mixed-race identity for the first time: "Well, I put Native American (although also Anglo, Spanish) cause I am almost half—3/8 and figure I like the government to know that we survived and are still kicking. Then, I had no compunction about putting Melungeon under other." Another individual shares her reasoning for identifying as Native American for the first time: "I filled out my short form and for the first time ever at age 64 . . . I answered American Indian, because we have always been told by the eldest members of our families, our Mother and my Grandmother, that we descended from American Indian. Hope this helps someone make up their mind."

Responding to the antagonism about the census, Wayne Winkler offers insight on the Melungeon discussion list into why it is important to fill out the census and why individuals should think carefully about self-designating as Melungeon:

> The census helps your community get money for their fire departments, money for the schools, and many other areas by determining the needs of the citizens according to what they put on the return. So, if you fail to answer questions, you are denying your community some much needed funding. There is no hidden agenda as far as I can tell AND the census will not be open for viewing by anyone for 70 some years and by then who cares? But if you want to put 'Other—Melungeon' on the census, ask yourself in what culture you were raised. Were you raised as a white person? If you recall the 1940's, '50's and early '60's, did you have the freedom to drink at any water fountain, sit in any restaurant, attend good schools, etc.? If so, do you really think that the discovery that you might have a few genetic components from non-white ancestors changes who and what you are? Finally, ask yourself this: is claiming this designation respectful to those who have not enjoyed the benefits of being 'white' in America?

Heritage and History

Following the publication of Kennedy's 1994 book *The Melungeons*, the rhetoric on the historical subjugation of Melungeons gained a new intensity. Kennedy writes: "The land-hungry Scots-Irish assigned to the Melungeons a fictitious heritage that suited their territorial designs, and then proceeded to forcibly confiscate Melungeon land. . . . [The] very presence of the Melungeons was effectively excised from all major history books and they as a people, were conveniently 'mystified' to further justify the inhumane treatment dealt them." (Kennedy 1992). Kennedy rallies his audience with descriptions of Melungeons as victim to a "tangled, sordid history of racism, disenfranchisement and forced displacement." He went on, "The same northern European hubris that first justified black slavery then perpetuated white racist attitudes" (Kennedy 1994b). Through Kennedy's voice, concepts like ethnic cleansing and cultural rape entered the vocabulary of the Melungeon story. As Kennedy raised the stakes in the dialogue on Melungeon oppression, the corollary line of reasoning that Melungeons overcame that oppression emerged. Kennedy himself immediately follows his telling of the sad story of the Melungeons with the rejoinder, "It proves we can overcome anything" (Napier 1995).

This combined sentiment of cultural tyranny and triumph is, perhaps, the most commonly echoed theme among Melungeon descendants. Individuals in the Melungeon movement play on a collective historical memory of hardship, rebellion, and survival when asked what it means to be Melungeon. Typical responses often include terms such as wise, hardworking, proud, honorable, and oppressed. When asked how they would define Melungeons to future generations, respondents elaborate on this language of oppression and resilience:

I am part of a group of people who survived against formidable odds. It is in our genes to survive and endure.

As pioneers of the Appalachian mountains who worked together in order to survive.

Misunderstood mixed race people (with Turkish or Sephardic Jewish ancestry) who have either struggled against many odds and much discrimination or have had to hide their heritage in order to avoid discrimination.

A mixed-race community either forced or voluntarily moved to greener pastures and probably stuck together for safety and survival.

A group of survivalists, a people who were mistreated — robbed of not only their homes, land and rights — but also of their identity, pride and dignity. They were a people who gave up who they were in order to survive.

Mixed breed people who lived happily in the Appalachians until/when a white supremacy moved in causing them to "run for the hills" to escape common white persecution and shame for being different.

A people of mixed race who intermarried, were ostracized, labeled, discriminated against, had their lands stolen.

I think it is to be of an interesting and diversified ancestry—a group of people who persevered in spite of adversity.

A brave, enduring people.

As is evident in the quotes above, pride readily transforms into a plea for historical disclosure and restitution. Darlene Wilson, a speaker at Melungeon events, announces: "Our attempt is to rescue this heritage . . . and restore it to its rightful place in history and in the hearts of the people" (Mysterious Origins 1997). In more modest form, a Union participant echoes, "Don't need no land, don't need no money, don't need any of that junk. We just need history straightened out" (Bowman 1997).

Racism Once Removed

Most Melungeon descendants talk about prejudice in the abstract rather than as part of their own or their families' experiences. Asked if they had ever witnessed discrimination against Melungeons, the majority of participants report that they had not. While some simply answer no, more often than not respondents qualify their answers, explaining that they do not live in heavily populated Melungeon areas or in areas where Melungeons are obvious. Only three respondents recall racist incidents directed specifically toward them. One woman remembers being told, "You don't look like anyone else. You need to try to look like others." Another woman remembers being called "nigger" or "Pocohantas" as a child. A third respondent recalls being an outcast on the basis of her Indianness: "When I was a senior in high school, I moved from MD to OK. On one of my 1st days at school, I was asked if I was an Indian and being proud of the fact that I was part (didn't know at the time just how much I was) I answered 'yes' and then was shunned for the rest of the school year. Luckily, it was my senior year. Interestingly enough, I was shunned by the Indians as well since I wasn't all Indian. Go figure."

Others who remember discrimination typically describe incidents removed in time and place, particularly those that happened to relatives rather than themselves:

Question: Have you experienced/witnessed any discrimination against Melungeons? Explain.

Yes, my sister—kids in school called her "blackie."

My mother was quite dark growing up in the 1950s in the Doris Day country club era (my father was a doctor); she was literally shunned.

My paternal grandfather couldn't get a job once he brought family up the hillbilly highway to escape the coal mines . . . told he was "too Indian looking." My maternal grandmother was proud that she "passed" (until you see her in black and white pictures!).

My mother was very dark (especially when young) and called "gypsy" in a non-flattering way; she always wore long sleeves winter and summer and would not allow her children to sunbathe.

No, I myself have not but I have told about my grandmother's people thinking she married a "nigger" so they never had anything to do with her.

It is also common for individuals to consider discriminatory events in relation to their newly-discovered Melungeonness. Many of these incidents typically occur with family members, doctors, and on the Internet. Often these incidents involve a level of mockery toward Melungeon descendants for claiming a multiethnic and, potentially, black identity.

Question: Have you experienced/witnessed any discrimination against Melungeons? Explain.

A doctor told me there was no proof and would not consider my health problems.

I felt uncomfortable outside of Unions in restaurants, libraries, etc. because so many have negative thoughts about race.

When I tell people, they frown if I mention Indian (east or native) or black descent.

People accept me, if they ask my ethnicity and I declare African American, they look hurt and turn off or ask dumb questions.

Can't get a job due to my size or can't figure "what I was," race, people staring to figure out what I am.

Yes, there are many people who still think Melungeons are African American in origin and because of their feelings toward blacks, they don't like Melungeons.

On message boards, people being rude about differing opinions, thinking they know it all, and having a problem with a suggestion of black or Native American influences in a family we might have in common.

Recently on the internet, someone stating that I should check with Alex Haley for my ancestry.

My neighbor asked me if I was celebrating Kwanza now.

As discussed earlier, it is reasonable to believe that historical Melungeons experienced some degree of discrimination. In addition, being viewed as ethnically mixed or different in the United States undoubtedly invites a brand of discrimination that is both confusing and painful. At the same time there is a tendency among Melungeons as a group to conceptualize Melungeon identity in relation to ethnic discrimination and disenfranchisement, despite the fact that few individuals recall experiencing or witnessing such discrimination on a firsthand basis. While most Melungeon descendants openly acknowledge this, they do so with apologetic explanations if they have not witnessed discrimination. Among those who do recall discrimination, examples tend to reflect singular incidents in their childhood. Though such incidents cannot and should not be invalidated, it seems fair to suggest a difference between hurtful episodes of prejudice and larger systems of bigotry in the United States. For example the kind of discrimination respondents report after claiming a Melungeon ethnicity represents a vastly different context of choice than the racism experienced by many minority groups in the United States.

The difficulty with this incongruity is that the tone of tyranny and redemption in the Melungeon movement suggests a narrative of discrimination that does not appear to be consistent with any kind of collective experience among Melungeon descendants. Instead individuals borrow from the presumed misfortune of their ancestors to produce personal narratives that imbue a sense of meaning and connectedness in their own lives. This creation, in and of itself, is not necessarily a bad thing; all humans arrange history in ways that bring meaning to the present. And paying homage to the presumed suffering of past ancestors is not a feature unique to Melungeon descendants. However when idiosyncratic and decontextualized claims inform broader ideas about race and racism, then understandings of racism become increasingly generalized and depleted of meaning.

For example, when asked to describe a racist scenario (real or imagined), most respondents tend to be vague. One male describes a racist scenario as "When someone don't like you for some reason or another." A female respondent answers: "When people try to break up humans that is racist; we are all one." Other responses focus on perceptions of "reverse racism." For example, in citing racist scenarios, respondents answer with comments like, "Racism is conducted by blacks and whites," and "giving blacks special considerations." One woman characterizes racism as refusal among immigrants to acculturate: "I really don't like the people who come to America and speak their own language in public like they are talking about other people or making fun of other people. That's like talking in front of a deaf person and not trying to translate." Another woman describes her personal experience with reverse racism at length: "One summer when I had a perm and had been swimming a lot and I was very tanned; I took some college classes and a very nice young black man helped me with my schedule so I more or less had every class with him; at first he sat with me and was friendly until my tan went and my hair grew out straight; then he stopped sitting with me and never talked to me again; at time I was hurt." A surprising number of responses that focus on this idea of reverse racism are more reactionary in tone:

Racism can be imagined today and also comes in ALL colors when it does exist. It is racist to blame white dead males for ALL the problems some people see today, just as it is racist to exclude or deny a Negroid/black person acknowledgment in some way based solely on race alone.

I have a best friend who is male and black. We are very open with each other, because we love each other as friends. There is not much we could say to the other that would be offensive. We are in the same environment and can see things different. I am sure my friend has been discriminated against. I saw it happen but a lot of the time he will say I bet this was said or done because I'm black, and I would know firsthand that was not the case. I see more social class and disabled discrimination than any other kind of discrimination.

I am always amazed when I discover that black people are "racist" against the white race. Most of the blacks in my neck of the woods call their own race "nigger" when they are mad at another black person. A black lady I worked with once called me a racist. I quickly told her that it did not matter to me what color her skin was, that it is her morals that I disapproved of, that I would feel the same way about a white person. She would dominate the conversation in the break room telling us all that her mother had never been married, that she had never been married, and her numerous children all had a different father, that her several teenage daughters was making her a grandma every few months, she was the only one in the family who had a job, etc.

Television broadcast of black only TV shows, groceries labeled for Hispanics, Native Americans having their own tribal government and jobs advertised as Native Americans are given preference — any race complaining that unfair treatment is due to race.

To be sure, not all of the racist scenarios given by the respondents center on issues of reverse racism. At least one third of the respondents provide answers relating racism to judging people on the basis of their appearance, skin color, and ethnic background. Individuals mention racist jokes and language, segregation, characterizing entire races, racial profiling, hate crimes, and differential treatment in employment, education, and housing. Although not a majority, these individuals do provide a lengthy and sophisticated list of many facets of racism. Still, among individuals who have spent a great deal of time contemplating issues of race and discrimination, it seems somewhat counter-intuitive that larger numbers of contemporary Melungeon descendants do not reflect a more nuanced and comprehensive perspective on racism.

Again I am not suggesting that these perceptions of racism among Melungeon descendants are inconsistent with the larger United States population. Indeed it is not unreasonable to suggest that these responses might even be more empathetic than the general public. Certainly, in a few cases, this seems to be the case. When asked how learning about Melungeons changed the way one thinks about other people or situations, a few individuals respond that they now have more appreciation of or greater interest in other cultures with comments such as "broadened my perspective" and "more empathetic and tolerant." One woman expresses her dismay that "such bigoted ignorance still so vehemently exists." However only one man made specific reference to non-Melungeon ethnic groups, stating that "I'm more sensitive toward the effects of imperialism and minority rights (Mayas of Mexico, Palestinians, etc.)." A few respondents make larger statements about the complexity of race. For example a woman states, "I realize people are more ethnically and racially mixed than they might know or want to know." Similarly, a male reflects that "race is not as simple as it once was considered."

The handful of those who reflect on broader issues of

discrimination do so in rather oblique ways that hint at historical discrimination against Melungeons rather than discrimination toward other minority groups. For example one woman states that learning about Melungeons "makes me sad that so much discrimination has taken place in the past." Another reflects: "I feel sorry and saddened of vanishing peoples and wish they could continue their bloodlines." Interestingly two respondents acknowledge their changed attitudes toward ethnic groups while couching their own family histories within the experiences of those groups. In response to the question of how one's knowledge of Melungeons impacts their understanding of other people, one woman states that "I have always been sympathetic to the Native American situation and now find my own family had their struggles and discriminations." Another comments, "I was always very liberal—just did not realize that I was a minority."

Most interesting, in terms of responses to the question of how learning about Melungeons changed one's perception of others, is the excess of answers that explicitly show—in an intentional and, again, reactionary way—that the responders' perceptions have not changed at all. These responses are intriguingly similar, with individuals stating that their ideas have not changed, because they have always been open-minded.

> **Question:** How has learning about Melungeons changed the way you think about other people or situations?
>
> Does not matter to me. . . . I have always liked people of all races if they were good moral people.
>
> It has not changed the way I think about other people and situations; I was raised to be accepting and tolerant of all people and situations.
>
> It hasn't changed my ways of how I think of other people, their behavior can change the way I think of them.

It has not. I was raised with a broadness of mind by very intelligent parents.

It really hasn't changed the way I think at all. I was raised in an environment of tolerance and respect for all races.

These responses are interesting in that Melungeon descendants consistently deflect issues of structural racism — both historically and in contemporary society — with a more equivocal language of discrimination. Though a few mention the oppression of Native Americans, nobody specifically mentions African Americans, or other minority groups in the United States. Instead responses among research participants provide an almost defensive stance with regard to racial politics. Most evidence suggests that Melungeonness — despite being understood directly in relation to race, discrimination, and ethnic identity — embodies a convenient singularity that is not informed by structural racism, but, in fact, and without compunction, sidesteps it.

The Mediterranean Mystique and Multicultural Morality Tales

Expressions of Mediterraneanity in Melungeon identity provide an opportune resting place from the confusion of identity commitments. In the Jim Crow South, blackness has always been, and continues to be, problematic for Melungeon descendants. Whiteness proper involves more liability in the post–Civil Rights United States, and, wary of the label "wannabes," Melungeon descendants are cautious about their self-identified Indianness. Thus Kennedy's introduction of a Mediterranean identity provides a compelling mechanism for individuals to claim an ethnic otherness that connotes a cultural exoticism that does not sacrifice the privileges of whiteness. While playing on themes of whiteness, blackness, and Indianness, Melungeons incorporate a presumed Mediterranean heritage as a way of conceptualizing a racialized identity that is at once elusive and primordial.

When asked what it means to be Melungeon, respondents reply with phrases such as "synonymous with preserved" and "heritage viewed through history." When asked how they would define Melungeons to future generations, respondents include comments such as "persons of ancient lineage" and "the first boat people." Melungeon descendants have clearly internalized notions of mysterious and exotic origins in their personal and collective identity narratives. Indeed most responses to the question of how one would describe Melungeons to future generations include some version of nativity, mystery, and maiden voyages. One individual defines Melungeons as "a mystery—quite like the Lost Colony—something to celebrate, something that has contributed to the diverse land we have." Another states that to be Melungeon is "to have a very old American ancestry, to be part of many peoples, to have many old questions answered." In yet another response, a man characterizes Melungeons as "having ancestors that were in America before the 'pilgrims,' were considered 'different' by the 'pilgrims' due to their appearance and were forced to hide in the mountain country to be able to live their own way for various reasons."

The exotic origin theories that have saddled the Melungeon legend for so long are central to Melungeon descendants' understandings of themselves and their place in history. Mediterraneanity, in particular, has become an integral component of the contemporary collective narrative of being Melungeon. In this way Melungeon descendants establish a foothold in the unfolding of American history. This heady stance is fortified by a newly constructed memory of being on the right side of history as ethnic underdogs who suffered the cumulative ills of Native Americans, underclass whites, black slaves, and Mediterranean intruders. Similar to other white ethnic revivals, contemporary Melungeonness provides a welcome escape from the historical taint of the dominating white class.

In the process Melungeonness becomes a multicultural morality tale of color-blindness and racial unity. As Brent Kennedy entered into the public eye in the 1990s, he preempted Melungeon descendants' oft-asked question, "What is a Melungeon?" with a prevailing tone of, "It doesn't matter." Kennedy's message has been consistent, since the publication of his book, that Melungeonness is boundless, an identity that serves as a metaphorical platform for multicultural harmony. In an interview following First Union, Kennedy stated: "The central importance of the story of the Melungeons is that we are all related—all brothers and sisters. Racism has no place in our world. We may never be able to determine how the Melungeons came to be, or just exactly what racial types we're made up of. And if we find that in fact there were no cultural and genetic relation to the Turks, Spanish, etc.? Well, so what? Look at the good that's come out of the inquiry. Let's all pretend we're related and see what happens!" (Schroeder 1997). Melungeon descendants echo Kennedy's regularly repeated sentiment with enthusiasm. This became especially apparent when respondents were asked how being Melungeon changed the way they thought about themselves:

Made me look at my identity and made me look at others—I have relatives and cousins where I am "not supposed to" living in the U.S. As Brent said, "We are all brothers and sisters."

That we are all really one big family, the big family called the "human race." I feel comfortable with ALL races.

Has caused me to believe that we are ALL brothers/sisters, or strongly related.

I think it has made me much more aware of individual identity of others—a recognition that, indeed, we are all "one people of many colors."

> See us all being related to each other — all peoples descended from same human being.

The color blindness so replete in the ethnographic rendering of the Melungeon movement illustrates precisely the rhetoric of color blindness in the larger United States. The primary difference is that Melungeon descendants purport to be oppressed while dismissing racism against blacks. Thus the result is a distinctly warped type of color blindness. The quandary with color blindness, however, is that it perpetuates what Bonilla-Silva (2006) describes as a "racism without racists," whereby the rhetoric of color blindness renders impotent any dialogue on racial equity in a society saturated with structural and individual racism. Melungeon descendants demonstrate the dubious nature of color blindness by perpetuating a multicultural dialogue emptied of racial politics. Borrowing from popular histories of mysterious origins, Melungeon descendants invoke a collective imaginary that privileges a vague sort of trans-ethnicity captured best by a Mediterranean mystique. Still, attempts at this type of transcendent identity are deeply racialized, deploying implicit and explicit notions of blackness, whiteness, Indianness, and, ultimately, otherness.

CHAPTER 6

The Melungeon Core

To suggest that any individual grew up as a Melungeon is a misnomer since, historically, there has never been a self-identified Melungeon community. Still there are individuals directly descended from, and who spent their lives in, communities historically labeled Melungeon. For the purposes of this research, I use the term "core Melungeons" to refer to individuals who grew up in these historical Melungeon communities and hold direct genealogical ties to the original mixed-race groups who settled there. This chapter draws from fifteen oral history interviews to reflect the perspectives of this Melungeon core.

The second part of this chapter is devoted to my discussion with Brent Kennedy. Though I would not typically include an interview transcript in a book of this nature, I chose to do so with Kennedy for a number of personal and professional reasons. When I conducted a formal interview with Kennedy, we spoke for hours. We covered an immense amount of material that speaks to many issues in this book. From a practical standpoint, it seemed more expeditious to include the interview in transcript form rather than resort to a series of continuous long quotes. Also in this vein, I found it difficult to extract portions of Kennedy's quotes, as his reflections tend to be layered, complex, and interwoven. Kennedy's visibility in the media is widespread, yet he is necessarily reduced to a series of sound-bites. Researchers have the luxury to avoid that, and I am capitalizing on that luxury in this particular case because Kennedy is such a central figure in the Melungeon movement. Beyond Kennedy's well-known eloquence, I was struck by his forthrightness. Given the nature of my work, I nervously approached Kennedy. He fielded questions that were sometimes critical and sensitive. Although he had not spoken on the record about many of the issues we discussed, he did not hesitate to do so with me. In this sense, he was exceptionally loyal to his general assertion that the Melungeon issue should be a dialogue that involves every viewpoint possible. I am not suggesting that Kennedy's ideas were necessarily more profound than those of other respondents, but as he was the catalyst for the Melungeon revitalization movement, his thoughts — uncut — are an important part of the historical record. This is particularly true since my interview with Kennedy was one of his last in-depth interviews before his disabling stroke in December 2005.

On the Ridge

As thousands of individuals contend with a newfound Melungeon identity, they imbue a contemporary identity with meanings that are largely detached from the experiences of individuals directly descended from core Melungeon populations. When contemporary ideas about what it means to be Melungeon collide with the life experiences of those viewed as Melungeon descendants, a disconnect emerges that diminishes an already elusive identity. In my experience core Melungeon families on Newman's Ridge are curious about their histories and are interested in talking. Still, most individuals — by their own admission — present an identity whose difference from other Appalachians is slight at best, with self-acknowledged distinctions grounded almost exclusively in terms of social class. Suspicious of outside representation, few of these individuals feel at ease with the Melungeon movement's eager embrace of an identity about which such individuals are both curious and skeptical.

The fact that many individuals who grew up on Newman's Ridge do not have stories to tell reflecting any kind of experiential reality of "being Melungeon" does not mean they do not have stories to tell. It was certainly evident in my interviews that these stories are important to the tellers as a way to communicate their lived experiences. Under the cloud of the Melungeon mystery, many individuals feel that their stories — precisely because they are not distinctly Melungeon — are dwarfed by a larger Melungeon narrative imposed on them by the media and outside world.

Most of those with whom I spoke share memories of a childhood shaped largely by social class rather than ethnicity. When answering questions about their lives, individuals center their discussions on working the land, the importance of kinship, religion, community, and self-subsistence. Respondents spoke at length about the trials of working the land as children, typically as children of tenant farmers. Issues of identity were secondary to maintaining family cohesion, meeting obligations to landowners, and getting by. As one respondent put it:

> We expected no more than to be tenant farmers. So wasn't more expected than we were to be poor. Being a tenant farmer was tough. They literally worked us like slaves. And you would move, and move and move and move. I don't think there was any ruder, or unkind, people on earth than those folks who run those farms. They would literally work you to death. They would work us like slaves from daylight to dark. And they would never pay us. And almost everybody in the county who has these big monstrous farms, the tenant farmers made their livin' for them. Their children would stay after

school and play basketball, practice til after dark. And the tenant kids worked, worked, worked. They worked us hard. And the parents weren't really able to take their side. They weren't capable of standing up to them. We just worked and worked and worked and worked.

Another respondent also talks about the arduousness and hazards of working in the fields:

I had three hoes takin' to hoe corn that day. I was about to drop one of them hoes and I done hit myself on the leg right there. Took a whole big hunk. I looked down and said, well, it ain't gonna bleed, I'll be alright. Few minutes [later] I looked back down, my whole shoe was full of blood. So I run back to the house, washed all that blood off of it, raised that big hunk of meat up, put me a lot of salt in it, put it back down over, tidied up, and went on. My sister wouldn't let me hoe corn that day, said you stay with granny, and I'll go hoe in your place. Only time I ever had any bad luck.

Also from a family of tenant farmers, another respondent reflects on the issue of poverty, though—like many I interviewed—he is quick to point out that, at the time, the community members did not necessarily consider themselves poverty-stricken: "You was poor and didn't know it I guess. . . . I remember when I went to school I thought maybe I'd be backward, maybe we'd be shamed of taking our biscuits, and maybe feel bad, because we didn't have what they called light bread, loaf bread. . . . I guess looking back at it we were some of the poorest people but, really, we ate off the land. I don't know if that was poor or not, just a way of life."

Individuals also spoke about moonshining as a side form of subsistence for their families. One respondent explains the practicality of making moonshine for money, as well

as the role of the legendary Melungeon moonshiner, Mahala Mullins:

> Everybody made the moonshine to live. My granddaddy, see
> those rocks over there, he'd take corn and put corn down in
> those rocks and he had to turn the corn into moonshine. And
> it was a livelihood. My granddaddy went off to town and they
> caught him, and the judge said to him, if you quit making that
> moonshine, I'll let you go home. And he said to the judge, and
> this is in court records, if I quit making moonshine, my fami-
> ly quits eating. And the judge said, I'll see you. And sent him
> off. But the story behind Mahala was that all the guys on the
> ridge who were making moonshine . . . as soon as they got it
> made, she had a little extra money, like my granddaddy could
> get a run of liquor off, take it straight to her. She would take
> it today. He wouldn't have to worry about the danger of get-
> ting caught. She would pay him, and he'd go right off on to
> town and get what he needed for the winter months. . . . All
> the guys would drive in. . . . They knew that she had the best
> moonshine in town, used to it was a choice commodity. These
> guys knew how to make pretty good stuff, and the high dollar
> folks wanted pretty good stuff, so she would save it for them.
> . . . When you think of moonshiners, you think of Thunder
> Road, all that, but it was really just simply trying to survive.
> If you didn't turn that little corn you had into shine, let Ma-
> hala have it, you wouldn't make it through winter.

Like subsistence, religion existed formally and informally
among individuals I interviewed. Respondents speak pas-
sionately about the Presbyterian mission that established
a church and school in the Vardy community in 1890. As is
well documented in Overbay's (2005) book, the Presbyterian mission accomplished enormous strides in the Vardy
community, changing the lives of children and families in
the area forever. Even those individuals who lived on Newman's Ridge but were not officially members of the Vardy

school speak in glowing terms of the missionaries, Reverend Leonard and Mary Rankin, and their impact on the community.

At the same time that the Presbyterian church and school thrived, a more informal Pentecostal worship was common among many families. Several respondents recall growing up in families whose parents were deeply invested in Pentecostal gatherings that involved lively and celebratory singing, speaking in tongues, and serpent-handling. One respondent remembers traveling with his father as a young boy to the "big snake meetings" at the juncture of the state lines of Tennessee and Kentucky. This meeting point allowed snake-handlers to avert any one set of state troopers by simply crossing the state line:

> We would just jump in the car on Saturday evening if they would let us, and go somewhere. You know, that was really goin, that was goin to the Bahamas on the 1st trip. I was able, real early on, to know it had nothing to do with Christianity. My dad had a couple ol' copperheads over there, and he'd take them everywhere they went. I went with a pastor one night over near Harlan. We stopped at the preacher's house, and when his wife came to the door, she was literally beaten to death. Her eyes was black, and her lips were black. The preacher asked, he said, Haay sister Gibson, that's how he talked, what in the world matter with you? He thought she'd had a wreck or something. She told us that her husband had just beaten her to death. We left their house, goin on towards the church and the hollar, and I was kinda prayin, I thought, I'm smart enough to know that if there's anything in the world to havin these snakes, they'll eat this guy up tonight. I mean, two and two is four. The dumbest guy in the world woulda figured that out. And I thought, this guy's gonna die tonight if there's anything to this business. So we go on up to the church, and they start, and they come in with the boxes. And they get the

music goin. And it wasn't very long until this guy dives right in there, and he gets him out 2, and puts them on his shirt and puts them on his head, puts them all over him. And that was one way the lord helped me to know that it was all junk. He handled those things for a solid 2 hours. But the funny thing about it, we got back in the car, I said, Preacher, there's something wrong here, something wrong here. He said, you can't never tell that tale. But from there . . . I already knew, deep within, that it was all a hoax. Because dad and his buddy was so mean, they'd do anything and still handle those snakes.

Another respondent also grew up in a Pentecostal family that handled snakes. Catching copperheads with a home-made snake-catcher made of a long pole with a string rigged to close around the snake's neck, the respondent delivered the snakes to an uncle who brought them to the church. He describes the church and snake handling: "They taught you how to live good. They said, now don't put your hand in the serpent box if you ain't living right or they'll kill you. And everybody didn't handle them in the church. I mean, the whole congregation didn't handle the snakes, just a few, you know, they would be involved in the singing and what-not, testifying, but everybody didn't handle snakes." Having seen snakes bite his father, uncles, and grandmother, he is cautious about snakes today, though his belief in aspects of the Holiness church remains strong. He describes the process of being immune to danger through the anointment of God. He describes his own ability to heal the sick with anointed hands:

I have been anointed, my hands have been anointed since I've been a Christian. My hands get so numb from here out just like I don't have no hands. I reckon that's how the anointing gets on them. That's actually the lightness, when they get hold of them snakes, they just, I mean, it's like a rag almost, like I had no hands. . . . I seen a young man once, I don't know how old I was, anyway, I saw him one night in the church building, and the stove was hot. The stovepipe was red hot, and I saw him just put his arms around it and hug the stove, and it never burned him.

As a child this individual regularly shared his experiences in the Pentecostal church with the Presbyterians. He remembers telling Reverend Leonard about speaking in tongues, trying to persuade him that it was real. He also remembers realizing at some point that, while the Presbyterians were always kind and generous, his Pentecostal life was better kept to himself during Bible study. Of course folk beliefs surrounding religion and healing hold a significant place in Appalachian culture as a whole and were not described by respondents as practices that were necessarily unique to Melungeons. It is also significant to point out that all families did not necessarily practice the same folkways. As one respondent put it, "A lot of folks did handle snakes, serpents. My family didn't. We ran from them. We killed all snakes."

Melungeons Who?

A consistent, and somewhat confounding, theme in my interviews in Hancock County was that few remember hearing the term Melungeon before the production of *Walk Toward the Sunset*. They do not recall overhearing, using, or wondering, as children, about the term Melungeon at home, at school, or as part of their everyday lives. I probed in myriad ways to explore when and how individuals heard about Melungeons, or might have been identified as Melungeons, yet most respondents consistently remember having no sense of the term before the drama. Melungeon was not remembered as a racial epithet that families chose to ignore, nor was it a secret that echoed through the mountains among neighbors. The notion of Melungeon simply

The Melungeon Core

did not exist as any kind of salient category until the production of the outdoor drama.

Ironically the oldest individual I interviewed—roundly agreed upon as a real Melungeon who would have a sense of the Melungeon past—remembers only hearing "old tales about Melunyuns." In this case someone identified by others as one of the few living original Melungeons relays only hearing about Melungeons in a folkloric sense. The older men in the family spoke of Melungeons, but not in relation to themselves or anybody in particular—only in the colorful ways that Melungeons appear to have been talked about in the region in general.

Most often respondents state that they simply had no comprehension of the word as children, then continue with a more theoretical commentary on the current belief that the term would not have been talked about openly. One respondent comments: "It wasn't mentioned. . . . Probably I was almost grown because you didn't hear anything about it at home, you know, our people, our grandparents didn't talk anything about it because they thought it was . . . evidently, it must have been something, somewhere down the line, was bad, or they thought it was bad, but I'd say I was practically grown. . . . The Vardy people didn't talk about it."

This kind of disclaimer that past generations would have known more about the epithet, and the discrimination surrounding it, represents a common thread in all of my interviews with core Melungeons. Respondents were equally forthcoming about not having felt any kind of discrimination—again with the addendum that discrimination was probably much more likely in older generations. For example one respondent relates, "I know, when it comes to any kind of discrimination . . . I don't know how bad it was the generation prior to me. My family was never discriminated against." In a similar vein, another individual reflects: "If anybody ever discriminated against me, they did it in such a subtle way I never noticed it. At that age and that time, there were plenty of other reasons that people would not like a teenage boy, other than being Melungeon (laughs). You know, I never really noticed any kind of discrimination, never felt that, even to the point later, of saying, those people are low down, don't get involved with those. So I had to learn all that 2nd hand, and people didn't talk about it." One respondent dismisses the part of Jesse Stewart's *Daughter of the Legend* in which a Melungeon girl faces discrimination: "I read Stewart's book, and I thought, I cannot relate to any of that. . . . I could not relate to anything in that story. Like the people hating Melungeons. Course I never heard the word Melungeon so I didn't know any hate. I never felt that anybody didn't like me or anything of that sort." Another individual who recalls, "I didn't ever remember hearing that word when I lived there," also denies ever being treated differently: "There wasn't any, what you call, prejudice, or anything that I remember over there. Dark skin or something, there was no difference. No one didn't even think about it."

When pressed to think about any context in which the word Melungeon might have been used, one respondent speaks fervently about living on the ridge while attending public school: "Going all the way through school, I never one time heard that name. Never one time heard a grown-up use that word. Never one time heard any mention of anything like that. That could not be true and me and my family know nothing about it. I started down there in 1st grade and went twelve years down there. Never one time seen any form, any kind, any resentment." The respondent then talks about childhood friendships — and, later, romantic relationships — with individuals in the town of Sneedville from middle to upper class families, as well as the educational support available, pointing out that none of that would have been likely in a context of discrimination.

The Melungeon Core

When asked more generally if they felt or were treated differently by others, responses relate only to being poor. A few individuals recall awareness of themselves and/or their families being dark-skinned; in one discussion, one respondent remembers attempts to avoid getting darker in the summer:

> They, like myself, they would get darker. . . . Dad always wore long sleeves and his . . . from here up . . . his hand would be darker than mine right now. Of course, I'll get darker, that never gets dark [laughs]. Anyway, my mother, she was a Gibson, and they were all dark people. Everybody say I look like my mother. As kids, my mama told us we were Irish and Indian, that's what she always told us. Course that connects up to the dark. She always told me . . . she would tell us to wear a hat so we won't get dark. She called it not getting black. She said to wear a hat and long sleeves when you're out in the fields working. But we'd get dark anyway, darker.

In this case there was some apprehension about dark skin, though the individual who told the story spoke of a general knowledge in the family that they were part Native American. The person does not remember dark skin in relation to any kind of larger stigma or discrimination. Others who have any memory of darker skin, or looking different, relate it to working in the sun or to family stories of having Native American ancestry.

Only two individuals with whom I spoke recall learning about Melungeons with the publication of Worden's 1947 *Saturday Evening Post* article. Claude Collins recounts his experience with first hearing the word Melungeon: "I was going to the University of Tennessee in 1948, and I read it in a *Saturday Evening Post*. I read the article, and when I came home, I told my mother about the article. And there was pictures in the magazine of my relatives. So when I finished telling her the story, she looked at me and said, now, Claude, don't you name that word anymore. So I just kinda casted it out."

Claude's story offers the first tangible evidence in interviews I conducted that older generations did, indeed, share and suppress a knowledge of the term, Melungeon, and its negative implications. Only one other individual I interviewed presented a memory of hearing the term with the arrival of the *Saturday Evening Post* at her home in Hancock County:

> I think the earliest memory I have was in 1947. I think, perhaps, you've heard me talk about this. I was in school and, during recess, we would go down the hill from the school to pick up the mail for mom and dad. Usually my older sisters did that, but, for some reason, I did it on the day that the *Saturday Evening Post* came. I went and I got it and was sitting on the front steps of the school looking at it. And I got real excited, seeing pictures of people in there that I knew. And I remember the *Saturday Evening Post* magazine, the photographer who took those pictures. I remember his being there, even though I was only 5 then. I remember his being in Vardy taking those pictures and my wanting to be in the pictures. And my mom saying, no, get away, don't let him take your pictures. And I remember my mother got very, very upset, because I wanted to get my picture made. And she was upset about the article in the magazine. And she took the magazine away from me and kept it up til, I guess it was the late 80s, or early 90s, whenever I first started talking about being a Melungeon.

Although this anecdote suggests the existence of both stigma and a conspiracy of silence among older generations, I would add a cautionary note that questions about memory construction and representation might be raised, given the teller's youth at the time. Interestingly individuals report not fully questioning the occasional arrival of photographers and journalists, particularly in Hancock County, and not seeing the resulting articles until adulthood. When asked what they thought outside journalists were doing at the time, one respondent laughs and says they probably thought "Somebody just wanted a picture of some poor folks." Another individual adds that journalists coming to Newman's Ridge typically encountered a lukewarm reception: "When people come through there and people didn't want to talk to them, asking questions, you know . . . I wasn't old enough to really realize what it was about but I know people didn't want to talk to them." The fact that individuals might have been both sensitized to and sensitive about outside journalists makes sense in the larger context of media attention focused on Appalachian people. From the period of color stories to media depictions of Appalachian poverty and backwardness, the region in general maintained a healthy suspicion of outsiders with cameras.

The Melungeon Movement

The issue of media representation — in general, and particularly with the drama — presents a common theme in all of my interviews in Hancock County. Of course the media has long scoured the mountains for hillbillies who are barefoot, disheveled, and dirty. Interestingly images and ideas proffered by the larger Melungeon movement via annual gatherings and the Internet also raised questions about representation for individuals who grew up on Newman's Ridge. Some of these individuals have not attended the Unions at all, others have gone once or twice out of curiosity, and a few regularly attend and embrace the MHA. When asked about the larger Melungeon phenomenon after attending his first Union, one respondent reflects, "Yeah, I was surprised the 1st time, because it seemed like there were not a lot of Melungeons from here there." After attending a meeting, another person ponders, "Well, I guess I was shocked when I went up there because . . . I didn't see none of the people that resembled the Melungeon people. It just looked to me like they was trying to get on the bandwagon. That's the way it looked like to me and I'm not belittling anybody. It looked like they were just trying to grab ahold of something." It was not uncommon for respondents to react to the Melungeon gatherings with curiosity. When asked about the larger Melungeon movement, one individual comments:

If they wannabe, let them be. There's several people out there that has no connections to Melungeons at all that wants to be Melungeon. If they want to be, that's fine. And if they did DNA testing, that might prove that they have no connection to Melungeons. Course that might be a slam on their ego. So if they want to be, fine. Just let them go with that. And if they want to be part of it, just let them be a part. There's nothing to gain by being Melungeon except association with Melungeon heritage. . . . I don't know what people are looking for when they come to these meetings and they are trying to come up with answers. I don't know what they are looking for. Since we been doing research, it's certainly got people more interested. Cause they read these books, and they'll look at the lineage, think maybe I'm Melungeon too. You know how it is with genealogy. And there's such an influx of people that's come in here, trying to find their lineage and saying, you know, I may be Melungeon, I really may be. And I say, well, that's OK if you are. Is that what you'd like to be?

Another respondent reveals some of the humor with which core Melungeons reflect on the Melungeon movement when talking about visitors to Mahala Mullins's cabin:

And another really, really interesting thing to me is the number of people who are Aunt Mahaley descendants. And they come, and they stand on that front porch, just like it is some kind of holy shrine. And the looks on their faces. It has just been amazing. And we have laughed so hard, reading things on the Internet, going to the Aunt Mahaley house that was up on Newman's Ridge and to her gatehouse. And we rolled. Her gatehouse! That was the corn crib! What are you talking about? The gatehouse! That was the pigsty. All these huts going to her house and different people, we're going by the gatehouse.

Others are more blunt in their disdain of the Melungeon movement. Interestingly class issues surface for this particular respondent who is bothered by the idea that individuals in the movement do not represent the middle-class status core Melungeons have achieved:

> I go to these meetings, and I see these people from everywhere in the world, and I say, how in the world do they fit into this? They have a t-shirt on that says, I am a Melungeon. I don't understand why they want to be Melungeon, you know, some of those ladies, look to me like they need to wash and clean up. . . . Now that's the thing that bugs me. And, really, honestly, some of the time, I think, shoot, I'm a cut above this crowd, you know, having grown up the way we did, you kind of delight in moving up the ladder.

Another individual offers a more pensive reflection on the Melungeon movement:

> If somebody wants to be what I am, how can I help but take that as a positive thing, you know? I'm not going to say, well, your evidence is pretty skimpy. But I can understand, in a way, you know, people who have . . . especially if you are closer to this . . . and if you're a generation older than mine, you actually felt the community looking down on you, you know, right now would be a time you would be saying, yeah, yeah, you all want to be Melungeons. You don't know what it was like when it wasn't a good thing. Well, you know, I don't have any of that. I just look at it as . . . these are folks who have questions, you know, if they were to find out all the answers like, OK, I

have no connection to Melungeons but still claim to be Melungeon, I would think that is a little strange, but what does it cost me? Why should I be bothered by it? . . . Certainly, there are people that have no connection whatsoever that are trying to do this. I don't know how many. I don't think it's very many. And I don't think very many of those I saw years ago are still involved in it. They've moved on to something else. There are people searching for an identity. There are people who are just afraid that when it all comes down to it, they are just plain old white folks, and they don't want that. They want something that they think is a little more exotic. . . . To me I think it's funny, because I can't think of anybody less exotic than my family. I mean, somebody else might think so, but they're common as dirt to me.

As illustrated in the above quote, most Hancock County respondents reflected on their own families as being unexceptional when it came to understanding anything about Melungeon history. They typically viewed their experiences as unique in that they grew up in a closely-knit community with strong family ties and a communal ethic of hard work. Many of those whom I interviewed were not uncomfortable identifying or being identified as Melungeons, yet their understanding of that label was based on geography and socioeconomic class, peppered with vague notions of a mysterious background. While most respondents had engaged the larger movement in one form or another—visiting a Union, reading Internet discussions, fielding curious visitors like myself—being Melungeon did not appear to be a substantial part of the way they talked about their lives. It is unlikely that this reticence results from any lingering stigma. Indeed many of the respondents had participated in DNA studies and did not hesitate to report to me their mixed ethnic makeup. It was also clear that they had discussed their results with one another. Many addressed

The Melungeon Core

the fact that their DNA results reflected a (usually small) percentage of African American ancestry. Very few, however, appeared to view the DNA studies, the research interest, or the contemporary Melungeon phenomenon as having any significant impact on their identities or worldview. It may well be true that ethnographers are a generation too late to learn anything about core Melungeons. There is also the possibility that the oft-repeated notion of having missed the real Melungeons who would know more is another part of the mythical presentation of Melungeons.

A Discussion with Brent Kennedy

I had only talked with Brent Kennedy for brief intervals before I interviewed him at length on March 2, 2004, in Kingsport, Tennessee. The conversations were usually at a Melungeon Union, where he would spend most of the day shaking hands, talking to people, and posing for pictures. He always struck me as gracious in the face of an overwhelming amount of attention. To manage this attention, particularly in front of the media, Kennedy had his spiel—certain pat stories, jokes, and responses—all of the equipment that any public speaker carries. Some of that spiel is found in my interview with Kennedy, albeit in longer sequences. For example most people involved with Melungeons know about Kennedy's illness, yet his story is so fascinating, it becomes intriguing to listen to in detail. I also had the pleasure of talking to Kennedy over an entire afternoon which allowed us to move beyond many of the basics of his personal story.

In truth, this was the part—moving beyond the basics—that explained my nervousness as I walked into Kennedy's office. I suspected Kennedy knew something about me as I had written one critical article on the Melungeon movement (Schrift 2003). I was not disappointed. Kennedy had done his homework. As I got comfortable, he casually dropped most of my biography into the conversation, his comments generous and flattering. The fact that Kennedy was so likable made the prospect of asking critical questions more daunting but, as I came to find out, made the actual discussion smooth and engaging. By the time I left Kennedy's office that afternoon and called my husband to tell him about the interview, I sounded like a lovesick teenager. I wanted to rethink my research, wear a Melungeon pride suit, and travel to Turkey.

In reality I did none of these, but I relay this (somewhat embarrassing) anecdote to make a point about Kennedy's charisma. I came across this word a lot in my early academic life when I studied the personality cult of Chairman Mao Zedong, though I am not sure I fully understood it merely by rifling through old relics. With Kennedy, charisma seemed to be the only satisfying word to characterize his intelligence, eloquence, and charm. As a social scientist I had always associated charismatic leadership with the more negative undertones of cult movements. After meeting with Kennedy, however, charisma struck me as more complex, a characteristic that embodied a degree of manipulation but held a more genuine, self-driven passion at its core. In addition to the reasons mentioned above, I include my conversation with Kennedy in an attempt to communicate even a hint of that charisma.

MS: How do you feel about your position in the Melungeon movement today?

BK: My entire mission from day one was to thrust this out there and force people to look at it. That's really what it's been all about for me. And the more I can step back, the better. I mean, there are times when I felt like if I was run over by a coal truck, then it'd go right back to the way it was. I don't know if it really was that way, but it felt that way. Now I feel like if I was run over by a coal truck nobody would notice, and it'd keep going. And I think that's great.

The Melungeon Core

And, to me, you know, the Melungeon aspect is what's important. The Melungeons were the hub, the nucleus of this mixed race population. And I take a very different view than folks that I like very much, and I don't see Melungeons as two families on one mountaintop. And that's it. I see the kinship. The truth of the story to me, and the whole beauty of the story for me, is that these few people that identified as Melungeons are the tip of the iceberg. And, if you're willing to look at it, it illuminates this broad-based, mixed race, ethnic heritage that we have, very deep, and we haven't wanted to talk about. And that angers some people. But it's what gets me up in the morning, and what makes my lights go on, and I can't change that. To me that's what it's about.

MS: Were you aware of the term Melungeon growing up?

BK: Oh yeah, oh yeah. I don't remember probably the first time I heard it, but the first time I was conscious of it [I] was probably six, seven years old. And my parents would take me up to the swimming lake, and people would talk about the Melungeons, you know, that lived nearby. But I didn't know what it was. The first time it really, truly hit me, there were people called Melungeons living five miles from where I lived. I was probably eleven or twelve years old, and I had gone up to Bark Camp Lake, also in Stone Mountain area, fishing. And these two older men came out of the woods with these old shotguns, old-fashioned shotguns, and I was into hunting and fishing at that time. It was like something from the Civil War. And they had a young boy with them, a little bit older than me. And they were darker than, say, the typical people in the area. But they didn't say a whole lot, basically, asked me if I was catching anything and we talked for a while, and they went on. But there was enough difference about them that I mentioned it to my dad. I asked my dad, and he said, "Oh, those were the Melungeons, some Melungeons." And I asked him who they were, and he said, "Well, nobody really knows, they're just a different group of people." And I remember at that time, and I did ask my dad, and he remembers this, and I said, "But they look like Mommy." And they did. My mom was probably darker than they were. That was the first time that I really remember seeing people called Melungeons, knowing, finally, what they were, they were human beings, and, also, thinking clearly to myself, what's the difference? I don't see the difference here. Why are they called that, and mama is mama? And then it was probably a year or two after that, I saw *Lawrence of Arabia*. And it was like all these Melungeons, in my mind, running across the street, and, of course, some were African, Turks, and Arabs. And that had a real impact on me, and I went home and talked to my mom about that.

M S: So you were aware that your mother looked different?

B K: Oh, yeah. I had comments made all the time to me. My mother, my mother's family, were talked about. I'd get into it. I didn't fight much because of my size. I got in a fight in high school, because this one man called my mother a "ramp." I didn't know what ramp meant at the time, I just knew he meant it negatively. But, you know, I'd also get comments on how beautiful my mother was, so, you know, it certainly balanced out. But there were those who made snide comments. Yeah, growing up I knew there were differences.

M S: What is a ramp?

B K: It's just a nickname given to the Melungeons up on Stone Mountain. So when someone said ramp, you knew they were talking about the Melungeons, or vice versa.

M S: How did the term come about?

B K: I don't know. Nobody is really sure. There may be a German term that is associated that basically means scoundrel. Some early German settlers could have possibly called them that. One of the theories is that the name came from wild onions that grew in the area, because Melungeons used

The Melungeon Core

ramps in their cooking. So that's another theory, but it's kind of like the word Melungeon. Nobody really knows, and maybe we never will. But, whatever the reason, it was a name hung on a Melungeon-related people in Lee County, Scott County, and Wise County. I don't think it was ever put on the families in Hancock that lived in the mountains there.

MS: When you were growing up, did you talk to your mom about being Melungeon?

BK: Not about being Melungeon. The only conversation that we had growing up related to that was my curiosity about those men I talked about. And my own noticing that they looked the same. Yeah, there was one conversation now that you mention it, that I recall. And, actually, you can still get to the source on this. My mother's cousin, Shirley, is still living. She married a Moore, and his mother was a Sexton. And his family were Melungeons from Stone Mountain. And when they married in the late 1940s, and I did hear this story told as a little boy, Shirley's parents tried to talk her out of marrying him cause he was Melungeon, and they used that term, distraught that she was going to marry a Melungeon. I do remember that, but it wasn't a major turning point in my life. But I knew, growing up, with my mother, aunts, other members of the family, I knew, whatever the name was, that something was different. As a little boy, I tried to find out what it was. I thought, somebody surely knows why these Scots-Irish people look the way they do. Of course, I got lots of stories. I got lots of stonewalls as well. But I stayed after it, finally gave up, moved away, and got back into it in my late 30s.

MS: And you got into it through your illness?

BK: My illness, yeah. That was the sarcoidosis. I had a couple of other illnesses in my heritage, whether those bleed over into all Melungeons, I certainly wouldn't expect that, each family is different. But, for me, the sarcoidosis, and I had very acute sarcoidosis. I didn't know if I was going to make it or not. I was bedridden, finally worked my way to the wheelchair, and on and on.

MS: How long were you bedridden?

BK: Oh, probably bedridden several months. I was thirty-seven years old when it came on full force. It was coming on three, four years. But then I went to a wheelchair. I was consulting and, looking back, flying on an airplane in a wheelchair, you get a real sense of how people who are handicapped feel. And I thought this is the way I'll live the rest of my life possibly. And I may not live more than three or four years. And that changes your whole perspective. I'm grateful every morning that I get to step out of bed. . . . The disease is absolutely more common among African Americans in this country, 80 percent of cases are African Americans, and then 10 percent or so are Middle Easterners and Portuguese immigrants, and the remaining percentage among Appalachian whites in this region. So that's really what struck me. Not that sarcoid really proved anything, but it was a hint and, for me, that experience made me say, ok, you know what, maybe there is something to all this. And I want to know. Maybe some people would get better and not give it a second thought, but that's not who I am. For me, it was a catalyst.

MS: How did the doctors figure out what it was?

BK: At first, I went to an ER, and I'd been to a family doctor a couple of times at that point. I knew something was wrong. Actually, I'd worked at Georgetown University, and, this was 1985, I went to a physician there. They thought it was sciatica developing in both legs, probably stress, and basically said, "Take an aspirin and forget about it." So I did. And it didn't go away. It continued to get worse. So it had been coming on for some time. It really worsened early in 1988. It got to the point that one weekend . . . I had driven to a client in Montgomery, Alabama, and, on the way home . . . it was a miserable trip, physically, and I tried to hide it the best I could, but I didn't think I was going to make it to Atlanta. Made it back, went straight to bed, and the next morning I couldn't get out of bed. My wife, Robin, had to drag me down the hall, put me in the car, and drive to the ER, St. Joseph's Hospital. And that's where, finally, I was diagnosed. . . . A physician there with a lot of experience, a connective tissue guy, looked at all the welts I had on my body and saw they weren't mosquito bites, and he said, "Hmmm, I think you have sarcoidosis." And that's what led me to the diagnosis.

MS: Was he puzzled?

BK: No, he was not, because of his experience. . . . He told me some interesting stories. He knew, in this country, it was primarily African American, but he had practiced and done his internship in connective rheumatology tissue disorders in Cincinnati. And that was the first time he had seen sarcoid in any number among Caucasians. And he said to me at the time, "The Caucasians we are seeing it in are Appalachians, primarily Northern Kentucky." And they knew that. They couldn't figure out themselves why they were seeing it in this population of whites. He really changed my life, diagnosing me quickly and giving me steroids, and everything else they did. Six months later I began to go into remission, and it was wonderful. It changed my life.

MS: What were you treated with?

BK: There's not a whole lot they can do actually—steroids and colchicine. And colchicine was, actually, wonderful help. I've been on and off colchicine for a long, long time. I continued to have bouts of what I'd had before, sarcoid, and then I became more insistent to the fact that maybe everybody does not go through this with sarcoidosis. And I talked to some doctors, and they had no idea. Then, here in Kingsport, Dr. Chris Morris first suggested to me that I had the symptoms of familial Mediterranean fever. He started asking questions about my childhood, and I had these puzzles. Even as a kid, I'd miss little league games because of joint pain, all these things. And it would come regularly, come and go, come and go, come and go. So he sent me to the National Institutes of Health, and they worked up some things, and I don't know if we'll ever know what they found because it was a research study program. And the only way they treat it anyway is with colchicine. So they put me back on colchicine, and it was like, my whole life changed. I don't have the bouts anymore.

MS: Were these bouts of pain?

BK: Pain, fever, it would move up in my chest area. Sometimes I would think I was having a heart attack, and this would go back to when I was a little kid, just real aches and pains and hurting to move, and then it would settle into the shoulder, and then this shoulder, this hip, this knee. And I'd get these little rashes that would come up my lower legs up to my chest and shoulders which is typical of FMF. And I had been to doctors earlier [who] said it must be the detergent, change the detergent. I mean, it's a hard disease to diagnose. And, so, with the colchicine, I was like, how can this be? That it's that easy. And I've actually cut down now. I don't take colchicine every day. I take it once a week and that just seems to be enough to forestall the attack. And when I feel one coming on, I start feeling for no reason at all, it's like a hot flash. And if I feel that coming on, I'll go back on the full regimen and that seems to lessen it considerably. I think Chris Morris now has in excess of thirty patients in this area, and he's still working on NIH with that. You know, the thing with this is, from a health care standpoint, that's really my major interest, you don't have to be Melungeon or consider yourself Melungeon, and Melungeon's not a race. It's a cultural issue. But Melungeon can be everything. It can be Turk, Native American, Scots-Irish, it can be all these things rolled into one. But I think the important thing is that in the health

The Melungeon Core

care industry, we need to educate physicians nationally, and here too. Just because we're in Appalachia, don't assume that everyone who comes in with the name Kennedy and blue eyes is northern European — therefore, you never look for other answers when you're trying to diagnose a particular set of symptoms. And that's what we've done. And we, the people, ourselves, we get to take a big part of the blame. That's who we were taught that we are, so we have the names, and we've got the blue eyes, and we tell the doctors when they ask. We can't really blame them either. But our physicians need to look where there are "white folk" in this area that have sickle-cell anemia. OK, never rule that out. There are "black folk" in this area that have all the symptoms of FMF or other illnesses that we ought to think about.

MS: How do you think the medical knowledge will help us understand Melungeons?

BK: It's certainly helping on a human basis regardless of anything else. I think it's also helping from a historical basis in understanding that, if we have genetically-based diseases in this region, among these people, that we're supposed to have at a much higher rate than they should be, then it's a no-brainer. These people are more complicated, and complex, and mixed than we ever thought and, if that's the case, that leads to what really drives me and that is, folks, there ain't no such thing as race in the way that I was taught in the 1960s and early 70s in college. All these boundaries are blurred. We have ethnic groups, we have people who identify, perhaps, more with one group than another, but there's no such thing as purity. And you go back ten generations, and you got 1024 ancestors. Ten generations is back to the 1500s for most people. Don't tell me that you're pure anything. And I'm tired of hearing, you know, "I'm pure Scots-Irish, I'm pure Cherokee, or great, great grandma was a pure Cherokee princess." And

I understand the pride. I mean, we all want to belong, and I think that is an underlying element of the whole Melungeon story, you know, so many people want to belong. What is interesting to me about it, though, is that so many people want to belong to what I see as a broad-based mixed population as opposed to a very narrow triangle. And, of course, that's where some of the conflict arises. We absolutely have good people who want very much to be enrolled in a Native American tribe who consider themselves Melungeons. That's who they want to be. They wanna be Cherokee, or they wanna be Powhatan. And so you have some, I'm sorry to say, that do not want to entertain the notion of sub–Saharan African heritage. Well, maybe there isn't a large element of sub–Saharan African in their background, but somewhere along the line there probably is. I can tell by looking at a lot of my family that there certainly is. So what? So what? I mean, you take any single ancestor out of that mix, and you're not here. You know, if I have 30 percent of my ancestors and go back ten generations and there's sub–Saharan Africa from Angola, or whatever, hooray! I wish I could go back in time and meet them, you know. Because, again, if any one of them wasn't there, wasn't my ancestor, maybe I'd be Brent Kennedy, but I'd be a lot less fun Brent Kennedy [laughs]. I don't know. I'd be dead. I wouldn't have survived the sarcoid with a little less African in me, you know, since they seem to be the ones who suffered most from sarcoid.

MS: Why do you think your work resonated with so many people?

BK: You know it did, and I didn't expect that. Let me back up just a little bit and say, I never expected to write a book. I gathered as much information as I could, and I thought that, this is interesting, there's absolutely something here. And I was going back finding ethnicities claimed by various family members, and you start off as a Turk in

Southside, Virginia, and by the time you get to Grayson County, you're English. You're Portaghee in NC, then you're Portuguese Indian, then you're Cherokee, Scots-Irish, all in the same family. So, I thought, this is fascinating; surely somebody wants to look at this. So I peddled it, I mean, I went all through the South and Southeast to universities. Nobody was interested in it. I mean, very few people were interested in it in the way that I was. What I came to understand, first of all, it was such a broad topic and it's hard to categorize. It's not neat and clean. And there's also the racial element. And I didn't realize that at the time. I have a much better understanding of this now, that, a lot of folks were afraid of it cause you get into race, and it's like stepping onto flypaper, and people get angry. And there's a lot of emotion attached to it. So no matter what you do, you're going to make somebody mad. So I now see that that was probably a driving force. Plus people had their own projects. So, I finally said, I'm not a scholar. I'm a PhD but I'm still not a scholar. And I went ahead and did it, and I did it as a catalyst. And I knew that. I knew that. I told my wife at the time, "This is probably going to get me in trouble, but this might force the issue." And it did. But the other thing that it did was that it did resonate. And I got letters. I think what happened is that it did resonate with a lot of people here in the Southeast who had grown up like I had who had family members or themselves with a different look as so many in the Southeast are. We are a melting pot. But I think for a lot of the people at that time, it had been in the closet. We were not able to talk about it. Nobody cared. All they cared about was the perception of outsiders around them, and it was still a very racist society. So the older members of the family hid it. Those who knew, hid it. They didn't want to talk about it. And it had been hidden and submerged for so long, that even some of the older members didn't know it. So, the younger ones at that time, those in their 20s and 30s, who had been bothered by this or curious about it, they picked up on it and said, "You know what, yeah, I've been there. I know exactly what this guy is talking about." So they turned around and started looking at their own families. And I really think that's what happened. I think it caught some folks by surprise. It caught me by surprise. And I still don't know where the Melungeon story, per se, is going. I guess that I hope that it will continue to be looked at, and it will continue to serve, as sort of the lead ship, to understanding kinship.

M S: You talk a lot about Melungeons as one family that includes everybody. Do you think that such a flexible identity dilutes Melungeonness so that it is rendered meaningless or will be completely mocked?

B K: You know, that's an excellent question. I think it probably concerns the human need to strive to belong. And, so, if you are proud of this Melungeon heritage and you know you had an ancestor that would be considered Melungeon, that had suffered this or endured that, then you want to enhance that. You want to enhance your Melungeonism. For me, the beauty of this story for me is that we had these people referred to as Melungeons, or ramps, and they were thought to be a singular species. They never were. We can take pride in who they were, we can take pride in what they were, but the real beauty of this story for me is in keeping the memory of it and honoring it, but saying, look, the reality of it is, whoever they were in that time period, they were bits and pieces of many people who came before them. We are only bits and pieces of some of them. And the beauty is the interconnections. It is that spreading out. And what we're doing, I hope, is spreading it out from Appalachia. And I really want to connect with every other human being on earth. I want us to realize that, you know what, it is diluted. It's diluted all the way to Turkey, diluted to Africa, to Angola, probably, to Pakistan, it's

The Melungeon Core

diluted to east Asia, yeah, it is diluted. That's the point. We're one human family. Others will see it as diluted and, as you say, rendered meaningless. I view it as shared and becoming more meaningful.

MS: How do you narrow the definition of Melungeon down then to do research? I mean, there are people more directly connected to Melungeon ancestry and there are people forming a larger group attracted to if for various reasons.

BK: That's right, that's right. Yeah, I'm glad you raised this whole issue too. I don't see the two as being mutually exclusive. I think we have to keep searching for the original Melungeons. And we know the first time that we find them being talked about in a public way is probably in Arkansas in 1810 as Lungeons. And we know it was used in the Stony Creek minutes not far from here in 1813. But if that term was being used, was it being used earlier? We need to find out. Was it used in eastern Virginia, or western North Carolina? So research has to continue. And we need to continue to try to fine-tune everything we know about — what we refer to as — historical Melungeons. And so that has to continue. Years ago I proposed trying to create four categories. The first group would be historical, or original, Melungeons — those that we know. The second group would be Melungeon descendants. Third would be related Melungeons, kin basically. And the fourth group would be mixed-race people.

MS: I understand that, from the perspective of multicultural diversity, it's great that anyone can be Melungeon. But in terms of trying to find out something ethnographically about Melungeons, it becomes a lot trickier. I'm sure you had to deal with the same thing with the DNA tests, because you had to select a group of people to get DNA from.

BK: I think you need to break it down from an academic standpoint. And from a human standpoint too. I realize we can't just throw it all up in the air and everybody be happy. Life doesn't work that way, and it shouldn't work that way. So we need to do both. But we need to celebrate the kinship, and we need to recognize that some of the people stayed on the ridge, some of them left the ridge. The DNA presented an interesting challenge. What we did, what I did, was to try to pick people that would represent the historical Melungeons and, despite the criticism, we did that. I've gotten pressure, and on the list as well, to release those names. I can't do that, and they know it, so they love to beat up on you. And, what's interesting, some of them have gotten into their own studies—they're not releasing the names just like we couldn't. So what we did is that we took these samples, and we do have the genealogies, and we do know who they are. So we have a pool that is purely the Vardy, Hancock County, people. We have the Stone Mountain Melungeon families separately. We have those folks who consider themselves to be Melungeon descendants in the area as a group. Then we have Melungeon descendants who moved away as a group. And a group of people who are general Appalachians. Unfortunately it's not as big a sample group or control group as we'd like, but it's still something to go with. But the general Appalachian group is not included in Jones's preliminary results, and people know that. It's been explained, and most people accept that and understand it. But the problem is now . . . Kevin Jones was so beaten up on by three or four people in particular, he finally said, "You know, I don't need this." And he basically became incommunicado. He just is not communicating with people about it.

MS: Who was beating up on him—members of the Melungeon movement? Academia?

BK: No, no, no, not academia. There were some folks who said that the selection of those people—and they're right in a sense—that the selection of those people would dictate the results. And of course that's true. But I don't know any other way to do it. I think one of the criticisms was you should've only done four families. And my point was, all we're doing is MTDNA [Mitochondrial DNA] and the Y chromosome. If we do four families, we will only know the Y chromosome of Collins, Goins, Mullins and, I can't remember the fourth—we'll only know these four. What if the Melungeonism—whatever it was that made a Melungeon—did come through a male side, but was it a paternal grandfather? We're not going to know that doing it the way that you want to do it. We've got to take a broader sampling of the people in that community in that family. So we can separate them out. We can certainly look and see if Collins, Goins, Bowlin, Bunch, or what have you, turns out to be East Indian or African or Native American or what have you. That would be very telling for us. But what if they all come back northern European? That is not going to tell us what happened. Wouldn't it be nice, while we're doing it, if we get their paternal, or great, great, great paternal lines as well? Then we'll at least have them; we'll know. That's the approach we tried to take. The same thing with mitochondrial DNA through the female side. So we could take one line, but maybe it really wasn't the MTDNA that caused Mahala Mullins to be Melungeon. So our approach was to try to cast a net given the time period that we're in. And we did the best that we could, and we utilized the best available DNA technology. And it was free. It was given to us on a volunteer basis by Kevin Jones. But the problem, though, is that in the last four or five years, the ability to really fine-tune that has changed tremendously. So I guess my biggest disappointment is that whatever Kevin does now, it's only a hint.

MS: I can relate to Kevin's distress. It seems like there is no way to write about Melungeons without angering people.

BK: Well, I've survived it and I'm right here. But, Melissa, let me tell you, while it would do that, it would also put you in the company of . . . whatever may be thrown out there at you, whatever arrows, then you're one of six, seven, eight, ten, twelve and there is a certain strength in that. How do you plan to write about this?

M S: Now I'm in a position where I have a lot of information on the contemporary Melungeon movement. And I am interested in that as a reflection of racial politics today. So that's part of the story. It's interesting that we have this shift among people who no longer want to be exclusively white. And there are other questions that I'm interested in for people who grew up in Melungeon areas, but that probably depends on the access that I can get to people.

B K: I will tell you, years back, sitting down with some of the older folks in Hancock County, I didn't go in with a tape recorder, and I didn't go in with anything to write with. That was understood. They would open up, but they opened up because they saw me as someone who could go in and talk about the Mullinses in my family . . . and that's very different. Same thing in Stone Mountain and Coeburn Mountain. The interesting thing is, though, you're exactly right, there are some really wonderful stories there, and it is a major part of this whole phenomenon, but it really hasn't been told. And folks like Jean Patterson Bible and Bonnie Ball touched on it, but they didn't get into the families in quite the same way that someone like you would insist upon. We don't have that, and we don't have it in the recorded fashion. And yet, I lost one of my great aunts that had some wonderful stories, and, yet, I haven't published them. I haven't even written them down. And I don't know that I'm the one really to do it. And some of them really . . . they definitely impact on race and ethnicity, resentment, beliefs of who they felt they were.

M S: What new things have you learned about your own family history?

B K: Well, this goes back to a very important point of my

The Melungeon Core

book too . . . that is, the written records, census records, they don't tell the whole story. If you go back to that time period, 1700s, 1800s, the records probably tell very little of the story. What I now know, through the genetic testing, three of my four grandparents, we have Native American ancestry. One of my grandparents is 32 percent Native American, so, clearly, there is Native American there despite V. DeMarce's insistence that the records are correct. My mother's side, haplotype m, clearly in the Pakistan, south Asia area. We've got a number of u's. We have uk2 which is clearly Middle Eastern. So you start looking at all this . . . We're sub–Saharan African, we're everything, you know. My wife's family . . . their Native American is coming through east Asian. My Native American is coming through as Native American. So my Native American ancestry through this DNA print is showing up as the older Native American, those who crossed over much earlier. The Ojibwa side, Chippewa, is showing up as east Asian because they are from a different crossover, probably much later. There's this raging controversy, what is Native American? When did they come? Are they really Chinese? So where are we going to be five years from now, migrations and populations, I think it's just going to get more and more confused. Maybe the Melungeons played a role in kicking a lot of that off. . . . I think I wrote in my book "to bite and sting." I didn't realize that I would be bitten and stung a thousand times.

M S: How are things going with the Turkish connection?

B K: Well, the book just came out. It's really more of a reporting on what's happened and, without any confirmation or strong conclusions, but just saying, "This is what's gone on." I haven't had as much time lately to get to it, so it's probably not moved a whole lot beyond where it was two years ago. But I don't think there is any doubt . . . let me back up again. . . . When I first got interested in looking

at the heritage, I heard Turks from day one, but I discounted it. And one of the reasons I discounted it was because
I was working with several scholars at the time that said
that that is b.s., it's myth, there's nothing to it. There were
never Turks here, forget it. Even the Portuguese is a stretch.
But I had several people, too, that I mention in the book,
that stayed on it and kept pushing me. And I said, you
know what, the Turks probably were here. My first inclination was that they were conquerors and swashbuckling
Turks coming in. That's not how they came. They came as
slaves and servants and why wouldn't they have, because
they were going everywhere else in that time period and
that capacity. The French and Spanish were using them
as slaves, captured in battles. They were taking them to
the Caribbean. This is documented. I mean, why wouldn't
they have brought them here? And, then, I started looking at Jamestown and the records there, and, son of a gun,
there they were, you know, Tony the east Indian, Tony the
Turk. And Joseph the Armenian. As hard as records are to
find, if we have records showing the people are there, they
came and they stayed, maybe there is something to this,
you know. You know, Abraham Mullins, French Huguenot,
was my ancestor. I'm descended from him from six separate lines. Since 1692 this man has thousands of descendants in this area, throughout the Southeast probably. So
even if you only had a few Turkish families, and they had a
lot of children, you know, there could be quite a few genes
and oral traditions of having Turkish origins. So I assume
that, yeah, this is legitimate, why wouldn't it be, and the
deeper I dug, the more I thought it was.

MS: I have heard that the Turkish Research Association
is pursuing a connection between Turks and Native Americans. Are you involved in that?

BK: I have been to Turkey ten times and then it started dawning on me too, that we are simply looking for the

Turks in the Appalachian population, the Melungeon population. A lot of these people probably intermarried with Native Americans. And I brought this picture. . . . This is a young Turkish girl dressed in traditional Turkish attire from the 1500s from Anatolia. So, you know, the cultures were similar. So, why not? I mean, they were here. And then when I start thinking that way, I think, suddenly . . . well, linguistics can be very misleading. Lots of times things are just coincidence you know. You have to be careful there. But some of them go beyond coincidence to me when you look at, particularly, the eastern seaboard tribes that would have absorbed the Turks. When you have the same terms, like Anata, the immortal mother, in both Cherokee and Turkish language . . . so, I thought, there may well be a basis. So for ten trips and all the research we've done, I'm absolutely convinced that there is an Ottoman-Turkic connection to the southeast through Native Americans, through Melungeons, through good, blonde-haired, white-skinned Scots-Irishmen who are living today that have some aspect of heritage that came here in some capacity during the early settlement of the country. The other thing that is building through genetic work and more scientific work is that there absolutely is a connection, regardless of Melungeons, there absolutely is a connection between Turkic people and at least some Native Americans. One of the more recent findings, the Turks—and this is what's amazing—the Turks, since I've been talking with them for ten years, have been making the argument to me. They believe that many Native Americans are related to them through the Altia Turks. The Altia Turks are sort of considered the mothers and fathers of the modern Turkish people. The Altia Turks migrated down into what today is Turkey and then intermarried, peacefully or otherwise, with Jews, and Arabs and Armenians and Kurds and other people, which many Turks don't want to hear. And, then again, you['ve] got Turks with blonde hair and blue eyes and fair skin, saying they are pure central Asian, you know, I mean truly. But they intermarried and became the modern Turks, but they all go back to the Altia Turks. I had the opportunity to go to Turkey several times and meet and work with Altia Turks. And they look Native American. The Choctaw, Chickasaw Indian who's the eastern director of Indian Affairs was there for two trips, and he'll tell you. He was amazed at the similarities between the Altia Turks and Native Americans. Well, the most recent genetics work has now identified that the Altia Turks share with Native Americans the same basic four mitochondrial ABCD DNA. They're kin. Now, the question is—and this is interesting—which came first? And which direction did they go? Actually, some Turkish scholars now are saying, "You know what, we think maybe it's the other way around. Maybe the Native Americans did not descend from the Altias crossing over the Bering Strait. Maybe the Altias are actually Native Americans who came over, settled and became the parents of the Turkish people." That's one of the main things going on in Turkey. But the DNA is saying that it's there. Again, in very long-winded fashion, even without the Melungeons, there is a connection, undeniable connection, linguistically and genetically and, probably, culturally, from what I can see—and, again, this is anecdotal, from what I observed—between the Altia and some Native American groups. So that's still unfolding. I don't know where all that will end up, but it's going to end up in connections. And I don't address that in the book, because I didn't know it then. It was actually written, for the most part, two years ago.

MS: Do you plan any more delegations to Turkey?

BK: I don't know. We've been asked several times to go. Probably at some point, but most of those trips, people probably don't realize, most of those trips, we pay for, so, unfortunately, it's expensive. So I don't know that delegations

The Melungeon Core

are the way. I think we've established the contacts and the friendships. See, the Turks are tracking it another way too. Even if I were not convinced that we have Turkic heritage, I think that, for me, there's a lot of similar issues coming out in Turkey that have grabbed me as well—the Armenian issue, the relations with Greece, the mess that you have in Cypress. What I see when I go to Turkey is I see, basically, just exactly what we've been talking about, people who are related to one another who . . . Many get it and are trying to overcome it and others don't. You know, if you are Armenian, then you are not a real Turk. And that's insanity. I have a Turkish acquaintance that I've convinced to do his DNA and the sequence was absolutely clustered with what would be considered Armenian as opposed to what would be considered Turkish. And he was flabbergasted. In fact, I'd say he was a little bit angry. And we talked about it. And I think he's finally understanding, you know what, I identify as a Turk and that's OK. But how many Turks would find themselves so mixed if they did this and how many Armenians the same thing? So I've actually written some articles that, I think, will be published over there which will probably make some Turks happy and will probably put me on the bad list of a lot of the others about this very thing. But as we start looking more deeply, we're going to find that really just barely below the skin surfaces, that we're cousins. And to not understand that and to build these false barriers is insanity. I defy people to go to Istanbul and travel slightly west to the border of Greece and to cross the border back and forth and tell me what side they're on. Because the Muslim Turks on this side and the Greek Orthodox Christians on this side look the same. They're the same people divided by religion and false perceptions of who they are. So I want to cause some trouble there too. And I'm sure I will.

CLOSING THOUGHTS

Larry was one of the first core Melungeons I met in Hancock County. He is the son of evangelical, sharecropping parents. He grew up working the land on Newman's Ridge, alongside his brothers and sisters. Distressed from years of sun, his skin holds the patina of the legendary Melungeon—rugged, worn, olive. His face looks like a homegrown potato, folded and dimpled with curiosity and character.

I spent hours talking to Larry on his front porch. He talked about everything that related to his life as a child and adult and punctuated his stories with jokes, advice to me about raising my sons, and banter about Catholics, the media, and the government. He playfully boasted to his friends that an anthropologist had visited him a couple of times. "They knew it's Melungeon business," he said, and they laughed about him "getting studied." He told me this in the context of one of his favorite jokes:

> They were doin' a census in the mountains, and the census taker knocked on the door, asked the little boy, said, "Your dad home?"
>
> And the boy kinda talked funny, said, "Nope. Somebody killed him."
>
> "What about your mom, she home today?" the census taker asked.
>
> "Nope. Run off with a man."

Finally got down to say, "Is your brother home?"

"No, he's gone to Harvard."

He said, "What's he studyin' at Harvard?"

"Nuttin'."

"What's he a doin' there?"

"He's not studyin'. They're studyin' him!"

Though I never thought the joke was particularly funny (even after tracking down original versions), what was interesting to me was Larry's refrain after telling the joke: "So you're an anthropologist, and that's what you're doing. Studying me. Studying the brother at Harvard." I was never entirely comfortable with Larry's synthesis of our relationship. Still I admired his acute sensibilities regarding my presence and questions. Long saturated by outside interest in Melungeons, Larry did not withhold his well-honed skepticism.

Late one afternoon Larry's inquisitiveness about what I was doing got the better of him: "What do you think keeps driving you with this now? Your curiosity's just killin' you? Guess I'd ask you what in the world you're doin' this far from home, your drivin' force? You thinking somewhere in your genetic arena, you might be in there too?" I'm sure I looked at Larry with a slightly dumbfounded expression. I measured my response: "No, I don't think I'm a Melungeon. When I started this, I was living in Tennessee and wanted to do something local. When I moved to Wisconsin, I stayed interested. I'm not sure why." I felt some relief when Larry responded, "So, you're investing all your time and money and not just sure why. I ask myself that question too when I go to the [Melungeon] Unions. Why does it matter to me? And I don't know if I have an answer either. I guess just my curiosity and to see what's goin' on. Don't you ever ask yourself why?" "Yeah, I ask myself why a lot," I responded, thinking to myself, "more than you know and not just about Melungeons." Larry jerked me away from my neurotic philandering. "But what can you learn from talking to me? 'Cause you know, if you coulda talked to my granddaddy, you might have found something interesting, but what do you learn from talking to me?"

"Well, it's interesting to know what people *think* about being Melungeon," I offered. Larry was relentless. "What do you think that I think about Melungeons? Would you not agree that most folks pursuin' this Melungeon thing so much . . . it's just personal gain for them. The old folks say they're flickin' their lick. That's my take on it." I was beginning to have flashbacks of my most uncomfortable moments in academia: vicious red scribblings of "SO WHAT???" on a graduate school paper; a publication review that ended with a miserly, "This is so bad it boggles the mind"; a teaching evaluation in which a student demanded her money back. Academia is certainly no place for sissies, but I had yet to be accused of "flickin' my lick." I wasn't even entirely sure what that meant, but it didn't sound like a compliment.

My first instinct was to explain how little money academics made in general, and even less from their writing. Many local writers had produced books about Melungeons, though I doubted many of the authors were making substantial amounts of money as a result. Still I was aware that there was a status issue among Melungeon enthusiasts, regardless of how local the fame and glory. Larry continued: "Anyway, you're about twenty years too late. And twenty years ago, you would have been resented, because you're such a cut above the folks here. You know, if you'd have said you are an anthropologist from a university, you woulda blown everybody outta the water. That was so far out of our world that you would've got no information at all."

I attempted to engage Larry from a different angle: "Yeah,

plus going into somebody's house then, asking what it's like to be a Melungeon, I think it would have been like asking people what it's like to be mixed race or part black." This only prompted a shift by Larry to question other motives: "You guys, the folks that's workin' with you; they really want us to have that problem with the race deal, don't they? That's where I hear them comin' from."

With this, I felt momentarily defeated. Yes, I *was* interested in the race issue, and, academically, it was an interesting question. But was it the wrong question? Was it just irrelevant? Although I had struggled with many aspects of the Melungeon project over the years, I never doubted that perceptions about race were not an important issue. Most of the individuals I had interviewed to that point readily embraced the notion that Melungeons in general were mixed race, yet only a small fraction admitted that they, themselves, had black heritage. I thought back to my interview with Thelma in which her husband assured me that "there ain't no nigger in the woodpile here." As it happened it was not the only time that particular expression or racist language were used in my interviews.

I managed to find my footing. "I do think race is interesting, and I don't think that it is an issue manufactured by academics. I think, at some level, race always matters. When I talk to people who claim to be Melungeon, they talk about being mixed race. They want to talk about being Turkish, or Mediterranean, or Indian, but nobody wants to talk about being black. And that tells us something interesting about race in society." Larry commented that he didn't think it mattered to anybody in Hancock County if they were Turkish, Portuguese, or part black, but he didn't seem willing to press the point. Larry reflected briefly on his own DNA sample, admitting that he had expected it to "show more Native American" and that he hadn't expected "any black." He followed with, "It wouldn't have mattered."

Closing Thoughts

In truth my overall sense was that Larry's point was not disingenuous. Individuals in Hancock County with whom I spoke were not preoccupied with race in the same way that was apparent in the larger Melungeon movement. In part this might be explained by the fact that most of those with whom I spoke shared memories of a childhood shaped largely by social class rather than ethnicity. When answering questions about their lives, individuals center their discussions on working the land and on the importance of kinship, religion, community, and self-subsistence.

In contrast, when asked what it means to be Melungeon the overwhelming majority of Melungeon descendants related their newfound identities to ethnicity or race. At the same time few volunteered details with regard to a specific ethnicity or race. Rather than describing particular ethnic groups, respondents typically referred to Melungeons as "mixed" and "multiethnic," thereby forefronting the notion of ethnicity while remaining nebulous about the ethnic groups with which they identified. Indeed many individuals involved in the contemporary Melungeon movement hedged their bets in their own self-identification process, assuming a Melungeon identity with shifting and self-defining parameters.

To a great extent these parameters represent a collective narrative formed by the dual forces of two hundred years of media representation and Brent Kennedy's emergence as a public voice on Melungeons. Through the establishment of interlinking tropes, media from the 1800s to the present pose Melungeons as mountain-dwelling scoundrels who are both romantic and savage in their primitivism. Though some of the more negative connotations in these depictions changed over the years, the mysterious Melungeon endured, due primarily to the legend of exotic origins. While journalists appear to spot Melungeons every once in a while, their writing about them, upon closer examination, is typically a study in smoke and mirrors. The few ethnographers who have challenged this popular construction of Melungeonness have largely existed in the shadows of the larger Melungeon romance. A careful reading of reliable ethnographic sources, however, demystifies the Melungeon legend, and, instead, reinforces earlier ethnographic assertions that historical Melungeons were triracial isolates, or multiethnic populations of black, white, and American Indian descent who identified themselves on the basis of socioeconomic class, if at all.

This rather unpopular notion that Melungeons exist more as a legend than an ethnographic group has been dwarfed by more enigmatic media images, presented most notably in the 1990s by Brent Kennedy. Kennedy's presence served to revitalize the Melungeon legend in the form of a movement with actual people who were moved to question and unearth their own family histories. With dizzying speed the Melungeon movement escalated, resulting in thousands of people coming together on the Internet and eventually—through the establishment of the Melungeon Heritage Association—in person at annual Melungeon Unions.

Employing Kennedy's writings and other media as a template to fill in their own pasts, these self-identified Melungeon descendants often have little connection with areas understood as historical Melungeon settlements. Many invoke genealogy, blood quantum rhetoric, and physiological markers to fill in the gap, constructing an identity that both reflects and refracts media images.

Without denying the fact that individuals in the Melungeon movement have important stories to tell, I suggest, in this work, that the collective Melungeon story has become something much larger: a metaphor for racial politics in the contemporary United States. Similar to other ethnic revivals, the Melungeon movement draws from a socially constructed past of migration, hardship, and endurance. Also similar to other ethnic revivals, Melungeon identity construction is strategically racialized, establishing an ethnic hierarchy that prioritizes an off-white, Southern European otherness, phrased in terms of a Mediterranean heritage. This ethnic hierarchy reveals both distress associated with blackness and anxieties about whiteness. And as is often the case in identity construction in the United States, Melungeon descendants embrace Indianness. Stung by accusations among Native American groups of being wannabes, however, Melungeon descendants dilute this critique with claims to a Mediterranean heritage that carries a strong sense of cultural exoticism and rootedness. Mediterraneanity allows a partial retreat from whiteness at a point in time when whiteness, itself, is under critique and non-whiteness entails a broad symbolic capital. An identity that is loosely tethered in time and space, Mediterraneanity borrows from the past to create a new, racialized white ethnicity that capitalizes on the cachet of the cultural exotic while underplaying stigmatized aspects of heritage. Mediterraneanity accommodates an exotic otherness without sacrificing the privileges of whiteness. Melungeonness thus promises a skeleton key to identity, a purposefully amorphous "every-dentity" that seeks to occupy a new kind of space on the ethnic landscape.

Melungeon Questionnaire

1. Are you male or female?
2. What is/was your occupation?
3. Are you retired?
4. What is your total annual household salary?
5. Where were you born? (city, state)
6. Where do you live now? (city, state)
7. How old are you?
8. Are you single _____ married _____ divorced _____ widowed _____?
9. How many hours a day do you spend on the Melungeon mailing list?
10. How many Melungeon Unions have you attended?
11. Did you complete the 2000 Census? If not, why not?
12. If you did complete the Census, what ethnic category/categories did you choose?
13. Did this choice differ from the previous census? If so, why?
14. Do you consider yourself Melungeon?
15. What do you think it means to be Melungeon?
16. Where do you think Melungeons come from?
17. Did your parents consider themselves Melungeons?
18. How did others label you and your family when you were growing up?

19. When did you first hear/see the word, "Melungeon"? Where were you? How old were you?

20. When did you begin to think of yourself as Melungeon? Be as specific as possible.

21. Have you talked to your family or friends about being Melungeon? What did you say? What was their reaction?

22. How has learning about Melungeons changed the way you think about yourself?

23. How has learning about Melungeons changed the way you think about other people or situations?

24. What are your opinions about Melungeons being officially recognized as Native Americans by the government?

25. Are you actively involved in lobbying for such recognition? If so, how?

26. Have you experienced/witnessed any discrimination against Melungeons? Explain.

27. How would you describe Melungeons to future generations?

28. List physical and non-physical traits that you think of when you think of Melungeons.

29. List physical and non-physical traits that you think of when you think of Native Americans.

30. List physical and non-physical traits that you think of when you think of Black/African Americans.

31. List physical and non-physical traits that you think of when you think of White/European Americans.

32. List physical and non-physical traits that describe you.

33. List physical and non-physical traits that describe your parents.

34. List situations/scenarios that you would consider "racist" (these can be real or made-up events).

35. What do you call your problem? What name
    does it have?

36. What do you think has caused the problem?

37. When did your problem begin? Why do you
    think it started when it did?

38. What do you think the sickness does? How does
    it work?

39. Have you consulted a doctor about the problem?
    What did he/she say?

40. What kind of treatment are you receiving? What
    kind of treatment do you think you should receive?
    What are the most important results you hope to
    receive from this treatment?

41. What are the chief problems the sickness has
    caused?

42. What do you fear most about the sickness?

Media Articles

The following citations include media articles collected and analyzed in this research by the author.

Before 1900

1849

"The Melungeons." *Littell's Living Age* 20:618–619.

1889

King, Lucy. "The Melungeons." *Boston Traveler*, April 13.

1890

"The Malungeons: They are Nothing More than Mulattoes, Says a Correspondent," letter to the editor. *Nashville Daily American*, September 7.

Cartwright, J. A. "The Malungeons," letter to the editor. *Nashville Daily American*, September 10.

J. W. S. "Will Allen Defended," letter to the editor. *Nashville Daily American*, September 14.

Jarvis, L. M. "Advent of 'Melongeons' to Eastern Tennessee. A Strange People: Habits, Customs, and Characteristics of Malungeons." *Nashville Daily American*, September 14.

"The Word Malungeon." *Nashville Daily American*, September 15.

Baird, Dan. "A Backward Glance: The Light of History upon the Malungeon Tribes," letter to the editor. *Nashville Daily American*, September 15.

Ewing, R. M. Stories and Comment. *Nashville Daily American*, September 21.

"The Melungeons: A Peculiar Race of People Living in Hancock County." *Knoxville Journal*, September 28.

1891

Dromgoole, William Allen. "The Malungeons." *The Arena* 3:470–479.

———. "The Malungeon Tree and its Four Branches." *The Arena* 3:745–75.

1897

Humble, C. H. "A Visit to the Melungeons." *Home Mission Monthly* 11 (2).

"The Melungeons: Peculiar Race of East Tennessee, A Remarkable Woman," letter to the editor. *The State*, May 25.

"A Strange Tennessee People: The Malungeons and their Customs — Mystery of their Origin — Changes Wrought by Time." *New York Evening Post*, September 11.

1900–1919

1900

Smith, Lucious Evins. (ca. 1900.) "The Melungeon Girl's Duel." Typescript, McClurg Museum, Special Collections.

"Odd Mountain Race: They are Copper-Colored — Tennessee People who Claim to be Descended from Portuguese Colony had Trouble in Proving they were not Africans." *Chicago Record*, July 4.

1902

"The People of East Tennessee: They are a Puzzle to Ethnologists and are Called 'Malungeons.'" *New York Evening Post* (n.d.).

"Phase in Ethnology: Mr. James Mooney Investigates Early Portuguese Settlements." *Washington Post* (n.d.).

1903

Jarvis, L. M. *Hancock County Times*, April 17.

1910

"Who and What are the Melungeons? Mysterious Race in Mountains of Tennessee, They are not Whites, or Blacks, and they are not Descended from Red Men." *Nashville American Anniversary Edition*, June 26.
Amer, R. O. "Strange Folk of the Ozarks." *Nashville Daily American*, sec. 8, June 26.
King, Lucy. "Origin of Melungeon." *Nashville Daily American*, sec. 8, June 26.

1913

Shepherd, Lewis. "Romantic Account of the Celebrated 'Melungeon' Case (Interesting Reminiscence by Judge Lewis Shepherd of his Early Success as a Lawyer)." *Watson's Magazine* 17 (1): 34–40.

1920–1939

1923

"Distinct Race of People Inhabits the Mountains of East Tennessee, Is Different from all Other Races, Sinister and Mysterious Race of the Melungeons May Have Sprung from Phoenicians." *Kingsport Times*, August 7.

1924

"Newman's Ridge and the Melengens: Original Settlers Lived after Fashion of Indians, but Younger Generations have Advanced in Civilization and can no Longer be Classed as Melengens." *Knoxville Sentinel*, June 1.
Anderson, Douglas. "What Do You Know About Malungeons?" *Nashville Banner*, August 3.

1928

Gibson, Patton. "Says Melungeons are Phoenician," letter to the editor. *Knoxville News Sentinel*, February 2.

1936

Rogers, T. A. "A Romance of the Melungeons, Mysterious Racial Group in East Tennessee, Descendants of Phoenecians of Ancient Carthage, Subject of Dramatic Story Found in Memoirs of Late Judge Lewis Shepherd—Drama and Heartbreak Attended Early Lawsuit in which Chattanoogan Won his Spurs." *Chattanooga Sunday Times Magazine*, June 21.

1940–1949

1940

Crawford, Bruce. "Hills of Home." *Southern Literary Messenger* 2 (5): 302–313.

1945

Ball, Bonnie. "America's Mysterious Race." *Virginia Highway Bulletin*, April 1945, 2–3.

Peters, Mouzon. "Descendant of a Melungeon Won Celebrated Property Case Here." *Chattanooga Times*, June 17.

Ball, Bonnie. "Mystery Men of the Mountains." *Negro Digest*, January: 39–41.

———. "Who Are the Melungeons?" *Southern Literary Messenger* 3 (2): 5–7.

Addington, L. F. "Mountain Melungeons Let the World Go by." *Baltimore Sunday Sun*, July 29.

1947

Vincent, Bert. "Strolling—Melungeons Make News." *Knoxville News Sentinel*, June 18.

Leonard, Chester. Letter to the editor. *Saturday Evening Post*, December 20, 8.

1950–1959

1951

Weals, Vic. Home Folks. *Knoxville Journal*, July 24.

1952

Weals, Vic. Home Folks. *Knoxville Journal*, November 3.

1956

Vincent, Bert. Strolling. *Knoxville News Sentinel*, April 11.

1960–1969

1966

Yarbrough, Willard. "Figures Don't Show 'Wealth' of Hancock County." *Knoxville News Sentinel*, June 5.
———. "Hancock 'Fables' are True (Colorful Personalities)." *Knoxville News Sentinel*, June 10.

1968

Yarbrough, Willard. "Maligned Mountain Folk May be Topic of Drama: Hancock Melungeons." *Knoxville News Sentinel*, January 8.
Grohse, William. "Vardy." *Citizen Tribune*, July 11.
Yarbrough, Willard. "New Outdoor Drama on Melungeons Set." *Knoxville News Sentinel*, December 1.

1969

Hill, Ann. "Drama Will Tell Story of the Melungeons." *Johnson City Press Chronicle*, March 16.
Fetterman, John. "The Melungeons." *Louisville Courier-Journal Magazine*, March 30.
Glenn, Juanita. "Hancock Countians Prepare for Drama about Melungeons." *Knoxville Journal*, May 1.
Yarbrough, Willard. "Come Enjoy a Piece of History with Melungeons." *Knoxville News Sentinel*, June 29.
———. "Phoenicians or Lost Israel Tribe? Legends Vary on Melungeons." *Knoxville News Sentinel*, July 1.

————. "Trippers Take Melungeon Tour." *Knoxville News Sentinel*, July 2.

————. "Melungeon Story Part of State History." *Knoxville News Sentinel*, July 3.

Glenn, Juanita. "Hancock's Colorful Past Recalled with Artistry in New Outdoor Drama." *Knoxville Journal*, July 4.

1970–1979

1970

Glenn, Juanita. "Hancock Residents See Tourism as Greatest Hope." *Knoxville Journal*, February 24.

"Sneedville Drama Director Returns this Year." Tazewell, Tennessee, *Claiborne Progress*, June 18.

Fetterman, John. "The Mystery of Newman's Ridge." *Life Magazine*, June 26.

Yarbrough, Willard. "Visit Sneedville and Learn about Melungeons." *Knoxville News Sentinel*, June 28.

"Sneedville Drama Begins Second Season Tonight." *Claiborne Progress*, July 2.

Grant, Sandra. "They Work Here but Their Ties are Elsewhere." *Baltimore Evening Sun*, September 28.

"Jews May Have Beat Columbus." *San Francisco Chronicle*, October 19.

"Georgian Makes Connection Between Early Jewish Stones." *Knoxville Journal*, October 22.

"Mystery Surrounds Theories of Origin of Tennessee's Melungeon Clan." *Fort Worth Star Telegram*, November 4.

Bernstein, Carl. "Maryland's Brandywine People: Clan Scorned by Black, White." *Washington Post*, November 29.

1971

"Ernie Ford Heads Fund for 'Sunset.'" *Knoxville Journal*, January 27.

"'Jews Here First' Theory Bolstered by Mexican Stone, Professor Says." *Knoxville Journal*, March 23.

"Ben Harville to Direct Hancock Play." *Knoxville Journal,* March 25.

"Melungeon Story Director Board for '71 Headed by Governor Dunn." *Knoxville Journal,* April 23.

Nordheimer, Jon. "Mysterious Hill Folk Vanishing." *New York Times,* August 10.

———. "Most of the Melungeons are Either Gone . . . or Going." *Nashville Tennessean,* August 15.

"Melungeon Colony Fading Away." *Chicago Tribune,* August 19.

1972

"Melungeon Play Director Sought." *Claiborne Progress,* March 2.

"Drama Builds Melungeon Pride, Many Believe, Carson-Newman Details Support of Production." *Knoxville News Sentinel,* April 23.

Yarbrough, Willard. "Vardy Valley's Melungeons Last of a Dying Breed." *Huntsville Times,* April 26.

———. "Melungeons' Ways are Passing." *Knoxville News Sentinel,* April 26.

———. "Necessities are Luxuries for the Melungeons." *Johnson City Press Chronicle,* April 27.

———. "Seek to Direct Play on Melungeons." *Claiborne Progress,* May 4.

Taylor, Henry. "Scientists Solve Riddles of Antiquity." *Knoxville News Sentinel,* June 19.

"No Cast, No Crowd—Another Drama Fails." *Kingsport Times News,* September 25.

1973

Lynch, Jim. "The Melungeons: Who Are These People? The East Tennessee Mountains May Never Reveal the Secret." *Tennessee Magazine* 16(8): 3–5.

Head, Sterling. "Carson-Newman Aids in Drama." Morristown, Tennessee, *Citizen Tribune,* June 3.

Larue, Ric. "Hancock Hoe-Down: Sneedville Drama is Product of History and Hard Work." *Citizen Tribune,* June 17.

Stinson, Byron. "The Melungeons." *American History Illustrated*, November.

1974

Yarbrough, Willard. "Cumberland Gap is Due for Facelift: Emphasizing Place in History." *Knoxville News Sentinel*, April 7.

1976

Davis, Louise. "The Mystery of the Melungeons." In *Frontier Tales of Tennessee*, 165–179. Gretna LA: Pelican Publishing Co.

Alther, Lisa. "The Melungeon Melting Pot." *New Society* 15 (April).

Hodge, Tom. "The Melungeons: Descendants of a Lost Tribe of Israel?" *Johnson City Press Chronicle*, March 18.

1979

"History of Melungeons is Still Clouded in Mystery." *Denton, Texas, Record Chronicle*, October 28.

Yarbrough, Willard. "Hancock's Country Fair Provides Journey into Past with Melungeons." *Knoxville News Sentinel*, September 30.

1980–1889

1980

Yarbrough, Willard. "Mysterious Melungeons Add Appeal." *Knoxville News Sentinel*, May 11.

1982

Brewer, Carson. "Climbing Family Tree Brings Book Result." *Knoxville News Sentinel*, July 1.

1984

Paris, Barry. "Ridge Folks: Heirs to Uncertain Identity." *Pittsburgh Post Gazette*, December 31.

1987

Johnstone, Richard G. "The Mysterious Melungeons." Jonesville, Virginia, *Rural Living*, January: 24–26.

Canfield, Clarke. "Origins of Melungeon People Source of Mystery, Legends." *Nashville Banner*, April 27.

1989

Holyfield, Ida. "Recording History from a Sage's Point of View." Big Stone Gap, Virginia, *Post*, August 9.

1990–1999

1990

Brown, Fred. "Hancock Moonshiner was 'Catchable but not Fetchable.'" *Knoxville News Sentinel*, July 2.

1991

Floyd, E. Randall. "The Mystifying Melungeons: Great American Mysteries." *News Herald*, November 7.

1993

Weber, David. "Our Hispanic Past: A Fuzzy View Persists." *Chronicle of Higher Education*, March 10.

Howell, Rick. "Melungeons Settled Four of the Original Colonies." *Monroe County (Tennessee) Advocate/Democrat*, November 28.

1994

Harkness, David. "Crockett Legends Are Larger Than Life." *Knoxville News Sentinel*, January 12.

1995

"Little Known Ethnic Group in US Sparks Visit from Turkish TV Crew." *Nashville Banner*, November 17.

1996

Still, Kathy. "Melungeon, Native American Museum Opens at Norton." *Bristol Herald Courier*, May 24.

1997

Kennedy, N. Brent. "An Update on Melungeon Research." Online letter at http://www.melungeons.org (site defunct as of May 2012).

Schroeder, Joan. "The Melungeon Woodstock: A People Find Their Voice." *Blue Ridge Country* 10 (6): 36–43.

"CVC Hosts Melungeon Gathering." *Kingsport News Times,* July 3.

Tate, Suzanne. "Under One Sky: Melungeons Meet, Share during Wise First Union." Norton, Virginia, *The Coalfield Progress,* July 29.

Wills, Brian. "Melungeon First Union a Resounding Success." *Kingsport Times News,* August 3.

Goodyear, Mary K. "The Importance of Melungeon Research." *Appalachian Quarterly,* December: 80–82.

Davis, Marti. "Telling Tales for Children; Georgi's Simple Stories Paint a Picture of Pixies, Melungeons and Appalachian Folks." *Knoxville News Sentinel,* December 2.

"Watauga Pen Women Learn about Melungeon History." *Sullivan County (Tennessee) News,* December 11.

"Author Details Melungeon Heritage." *Kingsport Times News,* December 27.

1998

Wilson, John. "Pioneer Families; Bolton was a Melungeon Who Farmed Moccasin Bend Land." *Chattanooga Free Press,* February 1.

Anthony, Ted. "The Melungeons: Mountain Mystery, A Lost Society Becomes an Obsession for Man Searching Appalachia's Hills." *Huntsville (Alabama) Times,* June 7.

"More People Tracing Roots to Melungeons: Mountain People Still Cloaked in Mystery." Nashville *Tennessean,* June 7.

"Appalachia's Genetic Mystery: Who are the Melungeons? They Thought They Were Scots-Irish White Trash but

They May be Far More Exotic Than That." *Toronto Star,* June 14.

Anthony, Ted. "The Melungeons: Mystery in the Mountains." *Knoxville News Sentinel,* June 18.

"Traces of Lost Society Found in Appalachia." Sevierville, Tennessee, *The Mountain Press,* July 4.

Wilson, John. "Pioneer Families; Early-Settling Goings Family Intermarried with Cherokees." *Chattanooga Free Press,* December 6.

1999

"Melungeons Seek Tennessee Recognition as Native Americans." *Kingsport Times News,* January 16.

"Melungeons to Seek State Recognition." *Johnson City Press,* January 16.

"Citizens Ask to be Classified as Native Americans." Memphis, Tennessee *Commercial Appeal,* January 18.

"Melungeons, Others Want Recognition." Associated Press, January 18.

"Seeking Identity: State too Restrictive in Defining Native American." Associated Press, January 18.

Whitaker, Monica. "Clan Hopes DNA Proves Cherokee Heritage." *Tennessean,* April 15.

McNeil, Nellie. "Alther to Speak on Melungeon Mystery." *Kingsport Times News,* October 18.

2000–2003

2000

Johnson, Stan. "A Little Bit of History: Hancock Countian Enjoys Discussing Local History." Morristown, Tennessee, *Citizen Tribune,* April 16.

Killebrew, Libby Pearson. "Melungeon Attempts to Dispel Myths Stimulate Controversy." *Rogersville (Tennessee) Review,* May 10/11.

"Melungeon Third Union Continues Annual Celebration of Heritage." *Kingsport Times News,* May 17.

Hunter, David. A Little of This, Little of That From Email and the Mail Bag. *Knoxville News Sentinel,* May 30.

Marshall, Andrew. "Not Black or White but a Breed Apart." London, *The Independent,* June 4.

"Famous Melungeon Mahala Mullins Cabin Being Relocated and Restored." *Sneedville News Shopper,* July 17.

Veach, Damon. "Researching Texas Family With Twists." New Orleans *Times Picayune,* September 3.

2001

Kahn, Chris. "Mystery of Melungeons' Ancestry Being Dispelled." *Knoxville News Sentinel,* July 8.

"Appalachian Melungeons Use DNA as Evidence of Their Exotic Heritage." *Kingsport Times News,* July 8.

Hashaw, Tim. "Mysterious Melungeons: Tim Hashaw Reveals the True Origins of the People Called Melungeons." *Family Chronicle,* September/October: 13–16.

2002

"Melungeon Mysteries to be Revealed: Appalachian Descendants to Meet in Kingsport." *Citizen Tribune,* June 18.

"Long-Awaited Study of Melungeons Ready." Associated Press, June 19.

Kahn, Chris. "Melungeons Try to Clarify Heritage: Some Appalachian Families are Having DNA Analyzed." Associated Press, June.

———. "Appalachian 'Melungeons' End Ancestry Study." Clarksville, Tennessee, *Leaf Chronicle,* June 20.

Osborne, J. H. "Study Hopes to Unravel Mystery of Melungeons." *Kingsport Times News,* June 20.

Balloch, Jim. "A Question of Origins: Study Examines Melungeon Heredity." *Knoxville News Sentinel,* June 21.

Hooper, Ed. "Melungeon Mystery Remains Unsolved." *Star Journal,* June 28.

Balloch, Jim. "Melungeons Are Multicultural Not Racial Group, DNA Shows." *Knoxville News Sentinel*, June 29.

Brewer, Carson. "Melungeons were Reckless Riders, Colorful Dressers." *Knoxville News Sentinel*, July 14.

Goins, Jack H. "Examining Melungeon History through Genealogy: a Personal Journey." *Tennessee Ancestors*, December: 190–201.

2003

Brown, Fred. "Vardy Valley Tries to Preserve Lifestyle." *Knoxville News Sentinel*, March 23.

"Panel Discussion on Appalachian Indian Identity Scheduled." *Roanoke Times and World News*, March 31.

Morello, Carol. "Beneath Myth, Melungeons Find Roots of Oppression: Appalachian Descendants Embrace Heritage." *Washington Post*, May 30.

"Melungeons, Vardy Community Topic for Genealogical Society." *Standard Banner*, June 3.

"Lobby Support to Turkey from Melungeons." *Turkish Daily News*, July 26.

Undated Articles in Author's Possession

Anderson, Jack. "Poverty Thriving in Rural Appalachia."
Tiede, Tom. "Snake Hollow Loses the War on Poverty."

Hancock County Post Reporting on Melungeon Drama

1967

"Hancock Drama Group Moves Ahead." October 24.
"Outdoor Drama Study Proposed." December 7.
Grohse, William. "Resource Development Association Meets." December 14.

1968

"Drama Committee Meeting Set." January 4.
Bowlin, Corinne. "Drama Committee Meets." January 11.

Haralson, Ann. "Drama Plans Announced." January 23.

Conner, R. B. Drama News. February 8.

Turner, Charles. This is Your Town. February 8.

Grohse, William. "Resource Development Association." February 8.

———. "Hancock County Resource Development Association Meets." March 21.

———. "Hancock Resource Development Association Meets." April 18.

Haralson, Ann. "A Tour Through Hancock County." July 4.

"County Outdoor Historical Drama." July 4.

Greene, Alton. "The County That Time Forgot." July 4.

"Hancock County 'The Land of Enchantment.'" July 4.

"Melungeons." Reprinted from Tennessee Conservationist, July 4.

Grohse, William. "The Land of Mystery." Reprinted from *Tennessee Conservationist*, July 4.

"New Crafts Program at Mulberry." November 7.

Haralson, Ann. "Drama Group on Move." November 28.

———. "Dr. Hunter Discusses Drama." December 5.

———. "Construction Underway at County Drama Site." December 12.

———. "Community Cooperation to Make Drama Reality." December 26.

1969

"Craft Now on Display in Sneedville." March 6.

Bowlin, Dora. Drama News. March 20.

———. Drama News. March 27.

Berry, Janice. "Talent Needed." March 27.

Bowlin, Dora. Drama News. April 3.

———. Drama News. April 10.

Haralson, Ann. "Crafts Fair Saturday." April 10.

Grohse, William. "Support the Drama." April 10.

"New Outdoor Drama Opens in Sneedville on July 3." April 12.

Bowlin, Dora. Drama News. April 14.

———. Drama News. April 17.

"Fair Warning." April 17.

"Talent Show." April 17.

"Eat and Work at Drama Site." April 24.

"Working Bee Set." April 24.

Haralson, Ann. "Crafts Display a Big Success." April 24.

Grohse, William. Vardy Club News. April 24.

Bowlin, Dora. Drama News. May 1.

———. "Drama Still Needs Funds." May 8.

"Local Crafts Judged by Professionals." May 15.

Welton, John Lee. "Drama Tryouts Saturday at Elementary School." May 15.

Bowlin, Dora. "Drama Tryouts Reset." May 22.

———. Drama News. June 5.

———. Drama News. June 12.

———. Drama News. June 19.

———. Drama News. June 26.

Haralson, Ann. Crafts News. June 26.

Grohse, William. "The Land of Mystery." July 3.

Bowlin, Dora. "Hancock County The Land of the Beautiful Sunset." July 3.

"Melungeons." Reprinted from *Tennessee Conservationist*, July 3.

"Alex Stewart Works 'Old Timey' Way, He is a Master Craftsman." July 3.

"Welcome to Hancock County." July 3.

"Idea Followed by Hard Work Brings about Hancock County's Outdoor Drama." July 3.

"Legend of Melungeons to be Staged in Sneedville." July 3.

"Hancock County was Ready for its Many Visitors." July 10.

Bowlin, Dora. Drama News. July 10.

———. "Introducing the Cast of 'Walk Toward the Sunset.'" July 13.

———. "A 'Tribute.'" July 13.

———. Drama News. July 17.

———. Drama News. July 24.

"Drama Off to a Good Start." July 17.

Turner, Charles. This is Your Town. July 31.

———. This is Your Town. August 7.

"A History of the Drama: 'Walk Toward the Sunset.'" August 7.

Turner, Charles. This is Your Town. August 14.

"'Sunset' Successful and Rewarding." August 21.

"Well Done . . . Thank You." August 21.

Bowlin, Dora. "Hancock County Can Be Proud: 'Walk Toward the Sunset.'" August 21.

Turner, Charles. This is Your Town. August 28.

"Drama Season Highly Successful." August 28.

"Country Music Show Here This Saturday." August 28.

"A Promise of Greater Things to Come." September 4.

A Letter and an Article. September 11.

Breeding, Josephine Stone. "The Mysterious Melungeons." September 11.

"Quillen Discusses Grant for Drama." October 23.

"Shine Supports Drama Group." November 13.

1970

"Arts Commission Commends Local Drama." January 22.

"Sunrise Craft Association Will Judge Craft Entries April 17." April 9.

"Bruce Shine to Speak on Importance of Drama." April 9.

"John Lee Welton Will Direct Summer Drama." April 16.

Walko, Steve. "Paint Up, Clean Up, Fix Up Time Set." April 23.

Turner, Charles. This is Your Town. April 23.

———. This is Your Town. April 30.

"Tryouts for Drama Set May 9." May 7.

"Hancock Drama Association Honorary Directors Named." June 4.

"Thousands Due Here." June 19.

"Drama Seeks General Manager." June 25.

"Hancock County 'The Land of Enchantment.'" July 2.

"The Mysterious Race." July 16.

Turner, Charles. This is Your Town. July 16.

Other Reporting on Events in Hancock County, 1971–1973

"Artist Ed Bowlin Donates Painting to Drama Association." 1971. *Hancock News Journal,* March 19.

"Walk Toward the Sunset Goes to Legislature." 1971. *Hancock News Journal,* March 19.

"Hancock Drama Campaign Now Under Full Swing." 1971. *Hancock News Journal,* March 19.

"Hancock County Producers Announce Drama Auditions." 1971. *Knoxville Journal,* April 22.

"Drama Association Members Meet with Tennessee Ernie." 1971. *Hancock News Journal,* May 7.

"Senator Bill Brock to Attend Sneedville Play July 3rd." 1971. *Hancock News Journal.*

"Hancock Drama Sets Season." 1973. *Citizen Tribune,* February 1.

NOTES

Introduction

1. Three excellent resources on the history of the Lumbee are Sider (2003), Blu (2001), and Lowery (2010).

2. An enormous amount of work centers on Native American identity politics. Some of the most thorough and engaging ethnographic work can be found on the Lumbee tribe of North Carolina (Blu 2001; Sider 2003). For more recent non-Lumbee examples, see Sturm (2002).

3. A copy of the questionnaire can be found in Appendix 1.

4. A bibliography of sources that were collected and coded as part of this research can be found in Appendix 2.

1. Inventing the Melungeons

1. This quote comes from the title of one of the first and most influential stories among the color writers of Appalachia. The article was published by Will Wallace Harney in 1873 (Shapiro 1978).

3. Playing the First Melungeons

1. My summary of the drama is based on in-depth descriptions by Winkler (2004), Vande Brake (2001), and Ivey (1976).

4. Becoming Melungeon

1. This part of the questionnaire represented a modified version of Arthur Kleinman's (1981) explanatory model.

2. It is well beyond the scope of this study to unravel the nuances of DNA and/or the details of Jones's or earlier DNA studies. See Winkler (2004) for one of the best attempts at a lay overview of this work.

WORKS CITED

Anthony, Anthony. 1998. "Traces of Lost Society Haunt Appalachias." *Johnson City Press Chronicle*, June 7.

Aswell, James. 1937. "Lost Tribes of Tennessee's Mountains: Anglo-Saxons Found Melungeons When They Came to New Country." *Nashville Banner*, August 22.

Baldwin, Patricia A. Hopkins. 1996. "Few Agree on the Origin of Kentucky's Early Melungeon Settlers: Path of Mysterious Culture Winds through Kentucky." *Kentucky Explorer*, September, 35–38.

Beale, Calvin. 1957. "American Tri-racial Isolates: Their Status and Pertinence to Genetic Research." *Eugenics Quarterly* 4 (4): 187–96.

———. 1972. "An Overview of the Phenomenon of Mixed Racial Isolates in the United States." *American Anthropologist* 74 (3): 704–10.

Beaver, Patricia, and Helen Lewis. 1998. "Uncovering the Trail of Ethnic Denial." In *Cultural Diversity in the U.S. South: Anthropological Contributions to a Region in Transition*, edited by Carole Hill and Patricia Beaver, 51–68. Athens: University of Georgia Press.

Berry, Brewton. 1963. *Almost White*. New York: Macmillan.

Bird, S. Elizabeth, ed. 1996. *Dressing in Feathers: The Construction of the Indian in American Popular Culture*. Boulder CO: Westview Press.

Blu, Karen. 2001. *The Lumbee Problem: The Making of an American Indian People*. Cambridge: Cambridge University Press.

Bonilla-Silva, Eduardo. 1969. "Drama News." *Hancock County Post*, June 26.

———. 2006. *Racism without Racists: Color-Blind Racism and the Persistence of Racial Inequality in the United States*. New York: Rowman & Littlefield.

Bowman, Rex. 1997. "Blurring Boundaries: Melungeons Hope to Show Their Clan's Historical Contributions." *Richmond Times Dispatch*, July 27.

Brewer, Carson. 1970. "This is YOUR Community." *Knoxville News Sentinel*, August 2.

Brodkin, Karen. 1998. *How Jews Became White Folks and What That Says about Race in America*. New Brunswick NJ: Rutgers University Press.

Brown, Fred. 1990. "Hancock Moonshiner Was 'Catchable but not Fetchable.'" *Knoxville News Sentinel*, July 2.

Brunvand, Jan. 1991. *The Study of American Folklore*. New York: Norton.

Burma, John. 1946. "The Measurement of Negro 'Passing.'" *The American Journal of Sociology* 52 (1): 18–22.

Burnett, Swan. 1889. "A Note on the Melungeons." *American Anthropologist* 2:347–49.

Canfield, Clarke. 1987. "Origins of Melungeon People Source of Mystery, Legends." *Nashville Banner*, April 27.

Cavender, Anthony P. 1981. "The Melungeons of Upper East Tennessee: Persisting Social Identity." *Tennessee Anthropologist* 6 (1): 27–36.

Clark, Margy. 1969. "Keeping Alive the Melungeon Legend." *Kingsport Times News*, July 25.

Converse, Paul. 1912. "The Melungeons." *Southern Collegian*, December, 59–69.

Davis, Louise. 1963. "The Mystery of the Melungeons: Why Are They Vanishing?" *Nashville Tennessean Magazine*, September 29.

———. 1970. "Pushing for a Happy Ending." *Nashville Tennessean Magazine*, August 30.

Deloria, Philip. 1998. *Playing Indian*. New Haven CT: Yale University Press.

DeMarce, Virginia Easley. 1996. "Review Essay: The Melungeons." *National Genealogical Society Quarterly* 84:2: 134–49.

Drake, Richard. 2001. *A History of Appalachia*. Lexington: University Press of Kentucky.

Dromgoole, William Allen. 1890a. "Land of the Malungeons." *Nashville Sunday American*, August 31.

———. 1890b. "A Strange People." *Nashville Sunday American*, September 15.

———. 1891. "The Malungeons." *The Arena* 3:470–79.

Dunn, Peter. 1967. "Riddle of the Ridge: A Small Group of Dark-Skinned People Living in Poverty on a Mountain Ridge in North

Tennessee Have been Baffling American Anthropologists for Generations." *London Sunday Times Magazine*, January 15.

Eller, Ronald. 1982. *Miners, Millhands, and Mountaineers: Industrialization of the Appalachian South 1880–1920*. Knoxville: University of Tennessee Press.

Endicott, William. 1970. "The Melungeons: A Tennessee Mystery." *Washington Post*, November 16.

Estabrook, Arthur H., and Ivan E. McDougal. 1926. *Mongrel Virginians*. Baltimore: Williams and Wilkins.

Everett, C. S. 1999. "Melungeon History and Myth." *Appalachian Journal: A Regional Studies Review* 26 (4): 358–409.

Ewing, James. 1970. "Who are the Melungeons: Were Their Ancestors Ahead of Columbus and the Vikings?" *Tennessee Conservationist* 36 (7): 16.

"Fair Warning." 1969. *Hancock County Post*, April 17.

Finkler, Kaja. 2001. "The Kin in the Gene: The Medicalization of Family and Kinship in American Society." *Current Anthropology* 42 (2): 235–63.

Gallagher, Charles. 2003. "Playing the White Ethnic Card: Using Ethnic Identity to Deny Contemporary Racism." In *White Out: The Continuing Significance of Racism*, Ashley Doane and Eduardo Bonilla-Silva, eds., 145–58. New York: Routledge.

Garroutte, Eva Marie. 2003. *Real Indians: Identity and the Survival of Native America*. Berkeley: University of California Press.

Gilbert, William Harlen. 1946. "Memorandum Concerning the Characteristics of the Larger Mixed-Blood Racial Islands of the Eastern United States." *Social Forces* 24 (4): 438–47.

———. 1948. "Surviving Indian Groups of the Eastern United States." In *Annual Report of the Board of Regents of the Smithsonian Institution*, 407–38. Washington DC: Government Printing Office.

Glenn, Juanita. 1969. "Hancock Countians Prepare for Drama about Melungeons." *Knoxville Journal*, May 1.

Greene, Alton. 1968. "The County That Time Forgot." *Hancock County Post*, July 4.

Grohse, William. 1969. "Vardy Club News." *Hancock County Post*, April 24.

———. Grohse Papers. Tennessee State Library and Archives, Microfilm #501. Melungeon family data collected by Grohse prior to 1989.

Harkins, Anthony. 2004. *Hillbilly: A Cultural History of an American Icon*. New York: Oxford University Press.

Harper, Phillip Brian. 1998. "Passing for What? Racial Masquerade and the Demands of Upward Mobility." *Callaloo* 21 (2): 381–97.

Hartigan, John. 1999. *Racial Situations: Class Predicaments of Whiteness in Detroit*. Princeton NJ: Princeton University Press.

———. 2005. *Odd Tribes: Toward a Cultural Analysis of White People*. Durham NC: Duke University Press.

Harvey, Herb. 1951. "The Melungeons . . . Their Origin Remains Mystery." *Johnson City Press Chronicle*, April 22.

Hashaw, Tim. 2006. *Children of Perdition: Melungeons and the Struggle of Mixed America*. Macon GA: Mercer University Press.

Head, Sterling. 1973. "Carson-Newman Aids in Drama." Morristown, Tennessee, *Citizen Tribune*, June 3.

Henige, David. 1998. "The Melungeons Become a Race." *Appalachian Journal* 25 (3): 270–86.

Henshel, Richard. 1971. "Ability to Alter Skin Color: Some Implications for American Society." *The American Journal of Sociology* 76 (4): 734–42.

Herbermann, Maryann. 1994. "The Melungeon Mystique." *Mountaineer Times* 9 (2): 2–6.

Ivey, Saundra Keyes. 1976. "Oral, Printed, and Popular Culture Traditions Related to the Melungeons of Hancock County Tennessee." PhD diss., Indiana University.

Jacobson, Matthew Frye. 1998. *Whiteness of a Different Color*. Cambridge MA: Harvard University Press.

———. 2006. *Roots Too: White Ethnic Revival in Post–Civil Rights America*. Cambridge MA: Harvard University Press.

Kennedy, N. Brent. 1992. "The Melungeon Mystery Solved: Unraveling a Family's Heritage." *Blue Ridge Country*, July/August, 16–19.

———. 1994a. *The Melungeons: The Resurrection of a Proud People; An Untold Story of Ethnic Cleansing in America*. Macon GA: Mercer University Press.

———. 1994b. "Saga of the Melungeons." *Georgia Journal*, Winter: 18–21, 53–55.

Kleinman, Arthur. 1981. *Patients and Healers in the Context of Culture*. Berkeley: University of California Press.

Lowery, Malinda Maynor. 2010. *Race, Identity and the Making of a Nation*. Chapel Hill: University of North Carolina Press.

McDonald, Michael, and John Muldowny. 1982. *tva and the Dispossessed: The Resettlement of Population in the Norris Dam Area*. Knoxville: University of Tennessee Press.

McGowan, Kathleen. 2003. "Where Do We Really Come From? A New Generation of DNA Genealogists Stand Ready to Unearth Our Ancestors. We May Not Like What They Find." *Discover,* May, 58–63.

"Mediterranean Scholar's Theory Rekindles East Tennessee Melungeon Mystery." 1970. *Knoxville Journal,* October 20.

"The Melungeons." 1849. *Littell's Living Age* 20:618–19.

"Melungeons." 1981. *Knoxville News Sentinel,* April 26.

"The Melungeons: A Peculiar Race of People Living in Hancock County." 1890. *Knoxville Journal,* September 28.

"Melungeons Still Live On in Legend." 1987. Clarksville, Tennessee, *Leaf Chronicle,* July 20.

"Mysterious Melungeons: No Origin, No Color, At Last Tennesseans Finally Accept Them." 1970. *Bristol Herald Courier,* October 26.

"Mysterious Origins: Melungeons Meet to Share Lore." 1997. *Knoxville News Sentinel,* July 21.

Napier, Michelle. 1995. "Proud People: Kennedy Explains Melungeon History." *Scott County Virginia Star,* October 4.

Omi, Michael, and Howard Winant. 1994. *Racial Formation in the United States: From the 1960s to the 1990s.* New York: Routledge Press.

Overbay, DruAnna. 2005. *Windows on the Past: The Cultural Heritage of Vardy.* Mercer GA: Mercer University Press.

Peters, Mouzon. 1970. "Melungeons Steeped in Mystery, Many Theories of Their Origin." *Chattanooga Times,* November 29.

Plecker, W. A. 1942. Correspondence with Tennessee State Archivist, Mrs. John Trotwood Moore, cited in Winkler (2004), 137–42.

———. 1943. Letter to various county officials, cited in Winkler (2004), 143–44.

Podbers, Jacob. 2007. *The Electronic Front Porch: An Oral History of the Arrival of Modern Media in Rural Appalachia and the Melungeon Community.* Macon GA: Mercer University Press.

Pollitzer, William S., and William H. Brown. 1969. "Survey of Demography, Anthropometry, and Genetics in the Melungeons of Tennessee: An Isolate of Hybrid Origin in Process of Dissolution." *Human Biology* 41 (3): 388–400.

Price, Edward. 1951. "The Melungeons: A Mixed-Blood Strain of the Southern Appalachians." *Geographical Review* 41 (2): 256–71.

———. 1953. "A Geographic Analysis of White-Negro-Indian Racial Mixtures in Eastern United States." *Association of American Geographers* 43 (2): 138–55.

Price, Shirley. 1968. "The Melungeons Are Coming Out in the Open: Drama Pondered to Raise Their Name 'From Shame to the Hall of Fame' in Hancock County." *Kingsport Times News*, January 28.

Puckett, Anita. 2001. "The Melungeon Identity Movement and the Construction of Appalachian Whiteness." *Journal of Linguistic Anthropology* 11 (1): 131–46.

Rountree, Helen. 1990. *Pocahontas's People: The Powhatan Indians of Virginia through Four Centuries*. Norman: University of Oklahoma Press.

Schrift, Melissa. 2003. "Appalachian Melungeons and the Politics of Heritage." In *Southern Heritage on Display: Public Ritual and Ethnic Diversity*, edited by Celeste Ray, 106–29. Tuscaloosa: University of Alabama Press.

Schroeder, Joan. 1991. "In Search of the Melungeons." *Blue Ridge Country*, July/August, 22–25.

———. 1997. "The Melungeon Woodstock: A People Find Their Voice." *Blue Ridge Country* 10 (6): 36–43.

Scolnick, Joseph, and N. Brent Kennedy, eds. 2003. *From Anatolia to Appalachia: A Turkish-American Dialogue*. Macon GA: Mercer University Press.

Shapiro, Henry. 1978. *Appalachia on Our Mind: The Southern Mountains and Mountaineers in the American Consciousness, 1870–1920*. Chapel Hill: University of North Carolina Press.

Shepherd, Lewis. 1913. "Romantic Account of the Celebrated 'Melungeon' Case (Interesting Reminiscence by Judge Lewis Shepherd of his Early Success as a Lawyer)." *Watson's Magazine* 17 (1): 34–40.

Sider, Gerald. (1993) 2003. *Living Indian Histories: Lumbee and Tuscarora People in North Carolina*. Chapel Hill: University of North Carolina Press.

Smith, Jimmy Neil, and Olin Rogers. 1966. "The Secret of the Melungeons Buried Deeper Now as Progress Takes Toll of Mystery People." *Johnson City Press Chronicle*, September 18.

Sovine, Melanie. 1982. "The Mysterious Melungeons: A Critique of the Mythical Image." PhD diss., University of Kentucky.

Stinson, Byron. 1973. "The Melungeons." *American History Illustrated*, November.

Stuart, Jesse. 1994. *Daughter of the Legend*. Jesse Stuart Foundation.

Sturm, Circe. 2002. *Blood Politics: Race, Culture and Identity in the Cherokee Nation of Oklahoma*. Berkeley: University of California Press.

———. 2007. "Differential Passing and Indigenous Reclamation: The Racial and Cultural Politics of Cherokee Neotribalism."

Paper presented at the American Anthropological Association Meetings, Washington DC.

"These People Made a Pageant." 1970. *Trailblazer*, September/October: 12–13. (Copy in author's possession.)

"This and That." 1969. *Standard Banner*, July 12.

Tigue, Bill. 1969. "Drama Will Tell Story of the Melungeons." *Johnson City Press Chronicle*, March 16.

Turner, Charles. 1970. "This is Your Town." *Hancock County Post*, April 23.

Vande Brake, Katherine, ed. 2001. *How They Shine: Melungeon Characters in the Fiction of Appalachia*. Macon GA: Mercer University Press.

Vincent, Bert. 1964. Strolling. *Knoxville News Sentinel*, May 17.

———. 1969. Strolling. *Knoxville News Sentinel*, July 13.

"'Walk Toward the Sunset' Goes to Legislature." 1971. *Hancock News Journal*, March 19.

Waters, Mary C. 1990. *Ethnic Options: Choosing Identities in America*. Berkeley: University of California Press.

Watson, Sam. 1997. "Melungeon Ancestry: Family History Full of Mystery and Intrigue." *Johnson City Press*, September 21.

Whisnant, David. 1983. *All That is Native and Fine: The Politics of Culture in an American Region*. Chapel Hill: University of North Carolina Press.

"Why Have a Drama about the Melungeons in Hancock County?" 1968. *Hancock County Post*, February 8.

Winkler, Wayne. 2004. *Walking Toward the Sunset: the Melungeons of Appalachia*. Macon ga: Mercer University Press.

Worden, William L. 1947. "Sons of the Legend." *Saturday Evening Post*, October 18.

Yarbrough, Willard. 1968. "Maligned Mountain Folk May be Topic of Drama: Hancock Melungeons." *Knoxville News Sentinel*, January 8.

———. 1969a. "Trippers Take Melungeon Tour." *Knoxville News Sentinel*, July 2.

———. 1969b. "Melungeon Story Part of State History." *Knoxville News Sentinel*, July 3.

———. 1970. "Visit Sneedville and Learn about Melungeons." *Knoxville News Sentinel*, June 28.

———. 1972. "Melungeons' Ways are Passing." *Knoxville News Sentinel*, April 26.

———. 1979. "Hancock's Country Fair Provides Journey into Past with Melungeons." *Knoxville News Sentinel*, September 30.

———. 1980. "Mysterious Melungeons Add Appeal." *Knoxville News Sentinel*, May 11.

INDEX

disappearance, 66–68; journalistic writings, 34–49; on lawlessness, 61–63; manufactured legend by, 53, 87, 183; and outdoor drama, 76–81; and pilgrimages, 53–56; on primitiveness, 58–71; scholarship on, 51–53; tropes used, 52, 53, 76, 153, 183

Mediterranean origins, 10, 19–20, 52, 107, 136–39, 185

Melungeon Heritage Association (MHA), 2, 87, 90, 92, 95–96, 116, 121, 184

Melungeon identity: ambiguity in, 57, 90, 111, 169–70; and belonging, 109–10, 168–69; exotic origins, 1–2, 10, 19–20, 26, 52, 88–89, 100–101, 107, 136–39, 173–77, 185; and family secrets, 97–100; in Hancock County, 3, 6, 29–30, 35, 64–65, 81–82, 91, 156, 182–83; and illnesses, 88, 100–109, 163–64, 165; lack of, 97–99; of Melungeon descendants, 24, 30–31, 88, 90, 92, 110–11, 113, 127–28, 137–39, 183; as multiethnic, 2, 57, 90, 100, 113, 121, 165–67, 183–84; and Newman's Ridge, 4, 7, 24, 29–30, 47, 54, 72, 76, 79, 142–43; and otherness, 28, 33, 109, 136, 139; racialization of, 25–28, 136–37, 182–83; self-identification of, 3, 7, 16, 18, 24, 81, 87, 90, 92, 97, 184; social construction of, 3, 18, 22–23, 25, 87–88, 102, 105, 184–85; and white ethnicity, 28

Melungeon movement, 88–89, 153–57, 184

Melungeon Research Committee, 88

Melungeons: characteristics of, 37–40, 56–58, 60, 77–78, 100–105; core, use of term, 24, 141; cult of mystery around, 63–65, 68;

defining, 21–25; descendants, use of term, 24; journalistic writings on, 34–49; lawlessness of, 61–63; legend of, 2–3, 15–16, 23–24, 52–53, 87, 184; overview, 6–16; primitive isolation of, 58–61; research on, 18–19, 22–23; research process, 28–30; scholarship on, 16–21; use of term, 5, 6–7, 35, 37, 38–39, 64–65, 92–93, 148–49, 169

"The Melungeon Song," 1

MHA. See Melungeon Heritage Association

migration, Appalachian, 14–15, 91

missionaries in Appalachia, 15, 30, 33–34, 145

Mitrochondrial DNA (MTDNA), 171

moonshine. See whiskey distillation

Moore, Ms. John Trotwood, 11

Morris, Chris, 163–64

Morrison, Nancy Sparks, 100–102

MTDNA. See Mitrochondrial DNA

Muldowny, John, 14

Mullins, Abraham, 174

Mullins, Mahala, 30, 54, 144–45, 154–55, 171

Native Americans. See Indianness

New Deal policies, 13–14

Newman's Ridge TN: described, 61; and Melungeon identity, 4, 7, 24, 29–30, 47, 54, 72, 76, 79, 142–46; research on, 29

nostalgia, 15, 16, 67

Omi, Michael, 27

one-drop rule, 8

oral history, lack of, 22

otherness, 28, 33, 109, 136, 139

Pentecostalism, 146, 148

pilgrimages, 53–56

Plecker, W. A., 10–13, 15

Podbers, Jacob, 21

Portuguese origins, 10, 19, 174

poverty, 83–84, 144

Presbyterianism, 145–46, 148
Price, Edward, 17
primitiveness, 58–61

race: and assimilation, 12–13;
classification of, 8; and identity,
25–28, 136–37, 182–83; and
isolation, 52; multiracial census
option, 27, 124–25; perceptions
of racism, 128–36, 138, 182–83;
reverse racism, 132–34
ramp, use of term, 160–61
Rankin, Leonard, 146, 148
Rankin, Mary, 146
Robeson County Indians, 8–9
Rountree, Helen, 7

sarcoidosis, 88, 102–3, 106
Saturday Evening Post (magazine),
46–49, 151–52
Schroeder, Joan, 54
Scots-Irish population, 70, 102, 127,
161, 175
self-identification. See Melungeon
identity, self-realization
Shepherd, Lewis, 44–46, 57–58
shovel teeth, 100–105
snake-handling, 146–47
Sovine, Melanie, 19, 23, 49, 52
Stewart, Jesse, 150
Stone Mountain VA, 170, 172
Sturm, Circe, 27
surnames, Melungeon, 7, 29–30, 97

Tennessee Commission on Indian
Affairs, 114
Tennessee Conversationist (magazine),
75

Tennessee Valley Authority (TVA),
13–14
Third Union event, 1–6, 21–22, 29
Tigue, Bill, 77–78
Turkish origins, 1–2, 19, 88–89,
100–101, 173–77
Turner, Charles, 71, 75–76
TVA. See Tennessee Valley Authority

Unions, 1–6, 21–22, 29, 87, 92, 184

Vande Brake, Katherine, 21, 52
Vardy community, 30, 35, 54, 82,
145, 170

Walk Toward the Sunset (outdoor
drama), 69–76, 148–49;
community reception, 81–85; and
media, 76–81; story line, 79
Waters, Mary, 26–27, 109
Welton, John, 81
whiskey distillation, 48, 54–55, 61,
144–45
Whisnant, David, 15
whiteness: disillusionment
with, 27, 121–23, 185; and DNA
testing, 108; ethnic, 21, 26–27;
and otherness, 28, 109, 136; and
racialization of identity, 28
Wilson, Darlene, 128
Winant, Howard, 27
Winkler, Wayne, 20, 38, 47, 51–52,
82, 84–85, 126
Wirt, William, 14
Wise VA, 89
Worden, William, 46–49, 151

Yarbrough, Willard, 76, 81